Sail the Seven C's of Matrimony

SAFE HARBOR AWAITS...CHRIST IS YOUR COMPASS!

Published by Susan the Scribe, Inc.
www.susanthescribe.vpweb.com

ISBN is 978-0-9833848-7-8

Christian Marriage Homily & Ministry
Rev. Doctors Don and Anne Bloch
pairofdox2@yahoo.com

Publication Design and Layout by Andie Jackson,
Wonderdog Designs
 email: andiejax@att.net

Sail the Seven C's of Matrimony

SAFE HARBOR AWAITS...CHRIST IS YOUR COMPASS!

By the Reverend Doctors Don and Anne Bloch

With Susan D. Brandenburg

Cover Photo by Don Bloch
Lahaina Harbor, Maui, HI

Praise for *Sail the Seven C's of Matrimony*

"As someone who shipwrecked once on the high seas of matrimony, I believe the Bloch's book is a relationship life preserver."

~ **Victoria Register-Freeman**, Author of *Love Stories From The Bible*

"Over the last twenty five years, I have had the great privilege of personally experiencing the powerful ministry of Don and Anne Bloch. Their wisdom, Biblical grounding, and keen spiritual gifting have profoundly influenced and deeply touched my life … In *Sail the Seven C's of Matrimony* the Bloch's offer proven principles, hope, and practical help to navigate even the most shipwrecked marriage toward smooth sailing and calmer seas. Whether your marriage has veered just slightly off-course or has seemingly crashed on the rocks, these principles can and will bring healing and restoration….if you just follow the map they draw … the Bloch's have discovered the secret route that leads to fulfillment, joy, and true freedom in marriage."

~ **Nancy Stafford**, Actress (Co-Star of "Matlock") Speaker and Author of
Beauty by the Book: Seeing Yourself as God Sees You and
The Wonder of His Love: A Journey into the Heart of God.

"*B*eing a Navy veteran, I was inspired by the title of this book and how it related to marriage. What I found was a wonderful treatise on the core essentials of what it takes to make a marriage relationship sail and pull into its final port of a long life together. Just like the keel of a ship is crucial to the structure and strength of a sailing vessel, the Seven C's of Matrimony are the essential elements that give your marriage ship-solid strength and a structure that can weather any marital storms on the high seas of life."

~ **Richard D. Marks, Ph.D.**, President of *Marriage for Life*

"*T*he contents of this book are compact, yet transformative. Each of the Seven C's are practical to implement and have provided me with a renewed perspective for my relationship with my wife, Katherine. Thank you, Don and Anne!"

~ **Lance Sellon**, Team Pastor, CrossRoad Church

"*G*o ahead! Launch out into the deep waters of the Seven C's and see what happens. Don and Anne Bloch's practical, Biblically-based wisdom will make your marriage 'Sail!' "

~ **George Spencer**, Husband and Father, Counselor and Pastor, CrossRoad Church

"*G*od has fashioned some rare people to be comforters, guides, leaders, healers, educators, inspirations, comic relief, and timeless wisdom all at the same time. Don and Anne Bloch are two of these special people, uniquely brought together so that thousands may have the strength to reach out to Christ when they are battered by life's gale force winds. Time spent with the Blochs is always a welcome adventure. Anchors away! "

> ~ **Brian Niece**, Pursue Pastor at CrossRoad Church, UMC
> (Husband, Father, Preacher, Thinker, Teacher, Learner)

"*I* walked into a hospital room and found a couple struggling in the midst of their darkest day. I asked them how I could help. Together they said, 'To God be the glory for He is with us now and we hear His voice.' As we talked I learned that these two precious people were strong enough spiritually for this event in their lives because of the teaching and caring support for a Christ-centered marriage with Don and Anne.

I am delighted to be a part of a church that offers biblically-based and supportive training for young couples starting their journey into a Christian marriage. Don and Anne tirelessly provide this care. Their anointed ministry keeps our marriages strong and biblically focused. The fruit is strong families and a growing church. Let the Holy Spirit guide you as you read this helpful book. It will provide for you a way to tap into the resources that God has available to you for building your marriage. I am praying that you will enjoy your journey as you sail the Seven C`s."

> ~ **The Reverend Paul Wehr,** Retired Pastor & Elder, The Church of The Nazarene
> Member CrossRoad Church, Jacksonville, FL

Foreword

For several years, I had heard of the ministry of Don and Anne Bloch. I would have conversations with friends who would give testimony to the Blochs' love of Jesus Christ and their unique ability to manifest that love to others, bringing healing to emotionally broken individuals, marriages and families.

Early in the year 2000, a new couple began attending our congregation. After a few weeks they introduced themselves as Don and Anne Bloch. Over the next few months they began attending regularly and were selflessly offering themselves for service in our church. It wasn't long before I recognized that God used Don and Anne in unique and wonderful ways to heal broken people.

Sail the Seven Cs of Matrimony is authenticated by the life experiences of Don and Anne. The strength of this book is in the revelation of the weaknesses of these two individuals. They have both sailed some fairly rough courses in their lives. They have weathered the seas of criticism, bitterness, neglect, loneliness, rejection, and betrayal – the usual rough seas that all of us navigate. Through it all they have experienced the love of God and grace of our Savior and Lord Jesus Christ, revealed in a personal relationship through the Holy Spirit.

Although this book is written mainly to strengthen marriages, it goes way beyond that. It reaches to the core of all human need. There is something in each of us that is missing. There is a gnawing loneliness that we all try to fill in inadequate ways. We relate poorly to others because we relate poorly to God. We relate poorly in marriage because we relate poorly with God. We relate poorly with ourselves because, yes, our relationship with God is stormy.

To be very personal, I describe Don and Anne as *Relationship Junkies.* They thrive in relationships! They thrive while helping others build relationships!

It is quite humbling to be their pastor and to have them as a part of our ministry team. They are magnets for people who think there is no hope left for themselves, their marriages, or their families. They are compasses that point the way to our North Star.

I pray that you will be blessed as you read this book – blessed in the strengthening of your relationship with Jesus Christ, and, ultimately, in the strengthening of all your relationships.

Gee Sprague, Lead Pastor, CrossRoad Church, UMC, Jacksonville, Florida

Introduction

By Don Bloch

As a boy growing up in the city of St. Louis, Missouri, my first recollection of seeing anything other than scenes from the "asphalt city," was a first grade bus tour to a dairy farm in the country. My mother was one of the chaperones. As I stared out the bus window soaking up all the greenery, trees and farmland, my comment to my beloved mother was, "It's a great, wide, beautiful, wonderful world!" Even during the days when her life was ending here on earth, she always repeated those words back to me: *"It's a great, wide, beautiful, wonderful world."* I have always held on to that belief.

We are indebted to our God who often prodded me as early as 3 a.m. to write portions of this book. This is His work – not ours. Even as a small boy, God spoke clearly to me about how He would eventually use me for His glory.

At a conference, during a time of inner healing prayer, we were asked to recall an event in our lives that was a time of having fun! Then we were to invite Jesus into the scene to see what He would do with us. In exercises like this, my mind often returns to Forest Park in St. Louis, Missouri, where we made many visits to the zoo, the art museum and The Municipal Opera. We also spent long days sledding down Art Hill, sailing toy boats with my grandparents in the lagoon, wading in the waterfall near Skinker Blvd., canoeing with my mother in the lakes, and flying kites.

During this exercise, fond memories of kite flying flooded back. I connected the memory with the times that my maternal grandfather was in St. Louis's Jewish Hospital, which overlooked the park. As I was under age, I was not allowed to go to the room to visit, so in order to keep me entertained, a family member would often take me across the street into the park to help me fly my kite.

It was easy for me to re-live this scene of doing something fun! However, when Jesus was invited to join me, I wondered what His response would be. I was, after all, a little Jewish lad at the time and did not know Him. I assumed He would not have known me then, either.

In my inner being, to my delight, I saw Jesus holding the kite for me as I ran into the wind. Then, as we continued running, the kite really caught the breeze and took off! Wow! It soared to great heights – even to the end of the ball of string I held in my hand! So joyful was I at this accomplishment, I looked back to share the moment with my newfound friend, Jesus. He was smiling proudly at me. He said: *"You do not know me now. However, I will come back into your life at another time. Together, you and I will soar to much greater heights than this kite."* HE DID! WE ARE!

Dedication

We have not accumulated temporal financial wealth to leave behind for our family. We do, however, claim a much more important eternal legacy that we will leave to our children and their families. Since that life-changing event when our Messiah entered our hearts and brought us together in this ministry of love to hurting people, we have been blessed to witness our children invite Him into their lives and have seen Christian families emerge. The legacy we leave behind is Kingdom-living on earth and eternal life together with our Heavenly Father.

We, therefore, dedicate this book to our daughters, Bunni, Anne and Debbie and our sons, Steve and Randy. Our children have been fruitful and multiplied and blessed us with a total of twelve grandchildren and seven great-grandchildren! God's plan continues to unfold. We pray that all generations to come will be blessed with loving spouses just as we have been blessed with one another. We pray, also, that each of them will invite Jesus into the center of their marital relationships when the time comes for them to sail the Seven C's of Matrimony!

Don & Anne ><>

Acknowledgements

We were sailing into the depths of unchartered waters in writing our first book. It is, therefore, such an honor to acknowledge and give thanks to the following people who provided encouragement as they helped us chart the course with Jesus as our compass.

We are honored to give thanks and acknowledge our dear, valued close friend and extremely gifted writer, Susan D. Brandenburg, who took our writings and gave them her "Susan Touch", and our new valued friend, Andie Jackson, an incredibly talented graphic designer. Our Senior Pastor, The Reverend Gee Sprague, and our Pastoral Care Pastor, The Reverend George Spencer, also valued friends, who prayed with us that this book would bring glory to God.

We gratefully give thanks to those with whom we began our journey as conference speakers, where we witnessed numerous healings, including marriages. The Reverend Carl and Barbara Buffington, Bishop Phil and Jean Zampino, the late Ruth Carter Stapleton, the late John Wimber, The Reverend Terry and Ruth Fullam, the late Reverend Dennis Bennett and Rita Bennett. They have truly been Godly inspirations in our lives.

We are deeply indebted to The Reverend Francis and Judith MacNutt of Christian Healing Ministries who invited us to join them in moving their ministry to Jacksonville, Florida. Joining their incredible ministry is the reason we moved here from Kentucky in 1987. At the invitation of Bishop Frank Cerveny we began at Saint Johns Episcopal Cathedral with Norma Dearing until the MacNutts arrived eight months later. What a privilege, honor and blessing to have served God with them for many years.

We are blessed to acknowledge those ministers in Jacksonville who have also invited us to be on staff at the churches they serve. The Reverend Jay Hague, who asked us to be founders of Beaches Healing Ministry when Calvary Episcopal Church was established, The Reverend Bill Baldwin, Beach United Methodist Church, and The Reverend Gee Sprague, CrossRoad UMC, where we have been on staff for nearly fourteen years. We are extremely thankful to God for blessing us with these important people on our life's journey with the Lord.

Preface

The tiny boat tosses hopelessly in crashing waves, its terrified occupants holding on for dear life. Flashes of lightning pierce the sky! Thunder booms! The wild wind whips needles of rain into the desperate faces of the passengers, their shouts for help muted by the fury of the storm. It appears that all is lost.

Where is your marriage in the stormy, uncharted waters of the 21st century?

Jesus Christ stands in the center of the boat. He rebukes the winds and waves (Matthew 8:26). The storm subsides. With Christ at the helm, safe harbor is in sight. And safe harbor is just the beginning. Eternal joy is the true destination!

Why did you pick up this little book?

Are you contemplating marriage? Are you uncertain about your relationship with your future mate? Are you married and seeking to strengthen the bond with your partner? Are you sailing some rough seas right now in your relationship with your spouse? Are you thinking about divorce or separation?

You are not alone. God knows your needs. He has led you here.

There are seven major seas on this earth that God created. They are the Atlantic Ocean, Pacific Ocean, Indian Ocean, Arctic Ocean, Mediterranean Sea, Caribbean Sea and the Gulf of Mexico. Just as surely as God created those marvelous bodies of water, He has created the Seven C's of Matrimony that embody our relationship. As the seven seas flow from one continent to another, connecting our world, the Seven C's connect us with God and with one another.

Do you feel connected today, or are you floundering in a swirling sea of discontent and worry? In these desperate times of terror and trouble, with marriages and families drowning in divorce, the Seven C's of Matrimony are a life preserver thrown to you by Jesus Christ. With Christ as your pilot, you are about to embark on an exciting voyage of joyful fulfillment, regardless of where you are in your relationship right now.

Remember, God can reconcile any mixture! Even if you no longer get along with your spouse, think of what He did when He combined one molecule of a gas called oxygen with two molecules of hydrogen. He came up with a substance we cannot live without: Water! Then He took two deadly elements known as sodium and chlorine and came up with Salt! He can certainly take two opposing spouses and reconcile them to one another.

This is your port of embarkation. Climb aboard. Begin your voyage by listing all of the pros and cons of your present marriage or relationship.

You may be surprised to find that the pros outweigh the cons ... but, oh, those cons! If only things were different. If only he had a better job. If only she would lose weight. If only he would hold his temper. What if I had married someone else? What if he leaves me for another woman? He should take responsibility for his actions. She should work on her appearance. He should stop drinking. She should be more romantic. He should be a better father. She should keep a cleaner home.

The "if only's," "what if's" and "shoulds," putting conditions on our love, seem endless, don't they? A little play on words might be helpful at this point: Do not "should" on yourself ... Do not allow your partner to "should" on you ... lest you become full of "should."

OK. Do you have it all down in black and white?

TIME OUT! Take a deep breath and settle comfortably in a quiet place.

Where are you, physically, at this moment?

Look around the room and rest your eyes on an empty chair or sofa. Imagine Jesus sitting there. As always, He is there in the room with you. He knows what is in your heart and on your mind. There is no judgment in His eyes as He gazes at you – only compassion and unconditional love. Be still and know that He is there. Allow His love to embrace you and His peace to enfold you.

You are not sailing solo, even if your spouse has not joined you on this first step of the journey. Jesus is with you. He will help you to chart your course as soon as you begin giving Him permission to do so. By acknowledging the very real presence of Jesus in your own life and by allowing Him to guide you in your relationship with your spouse, you will be amazed at the results! Your cruise has left the port. The Seven C's await your arrival.

(Don): *Back in 1997, Anne and I flew to Boulder, Colorado to officiate at the wedding of my step-daughter, Anne, to Bob Hedlund. This was our daughter's wedding and I wanted it to be super special! I spent that flight in prayer for the perfect wedding homily. The Seven C's came into my mind fully formed as an answer to that prayer. Since God handed me that blessed homily for our daughter's wedding day, Anne and I have shared it with hundreds of couples.*

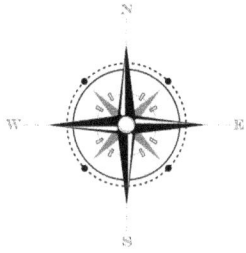

Table of Contents

Anne's Story:

I was raised in a small town in Oregon, an idyllic spot where one could look up and see snow-capped mountains and visit clear, cool lakes surrounded by lush, dark green pines. The beauty of the Creator was an ever-present reality. Within walking distance there was a small quaint church where I was sent to attend Sunday school. We never attended church as a family, nor was there prayer in our home. Even so, there was within me a certain kind of knowing that God did exist and that He loved me.

One day I asked the Sunday School teacher who that man was on the cross. When she told me He was Jesus and that He had died on the cross, I cried and cried as if my heart would break. At the time I knew not why. I do now, and am grateful beyond words!

As an only child of divorced parents, I suffered bitterly from the rejection of my mother and the distant coolness of an absentee father whom I adored. He left when I was eight years old without saying good-bye. I did not even know he was leaving. I wept daily, missing him desperately. My mother would find me crying and scold me, saying it was all my fault that he left us, and if it weren't for me, she would have a husband. That remark left me guilt-ridden and confused. She made it quite clear that she did not want me. "I can't stand the sight of you, you're exactly like your father." More confusion. I wanted to be exactly like my father!

At age nine, I had Rheumatic fever, and was bed-ridden for an entire year. My dad neither called nor came to see me. He crushed my heart once again.

The same was true when I was sent away to boarding school in Seattle, and again when I had polio my sophomore year of college. More crushes to the heart that longed for him to be in my life. All I ever wanted was for him to love me.

I became withdrawn and afraid to care for anyone because it hurt so deeply when they rejected me. I carried these insecurities into my adulthood.

1

My first marriage ended in a devastating divorce that shattered my heart. I was sent to Mexico to get a quick divorce so he could marry someone else right away. It was an incredibly degrading experience. I wanted, with all my heart, for him to change his mind. He did not see that happening. One positive thing did happen when my first marriage failed. I returned to Oregon with my two daughters, and the relationship between my father and myself was healed. What a blessing!

Seven years later I married my second husband, who was 15 years my senior. He was abusive verbally and physically, as was my first husband. He died quite unexpectedly in his sleep while I was away visiting my Aunt Anne in Wisconsin. Two weeks later, upon my return home, I discovered his lifeless body in our bed. The autopsy showed that he had died the day I left. Once again, I was devastated and ridden with guilt because I was not with him when he died.

Both husbands rejected me when I gained weight, a problem that started when I gave birth to my children. The more they rejected me, the more I ate. It became a vicious cycle.

Completely devastated by the events of my life, I plunged into the depths of despair, depression, self-hatred and guilt. I turned into an emotional and physical invalid, developing arthritis, bursitis, tendinitis and every other "itis" there is. My neck was in a brace; both arms in a sling; my hands so blue and swollen they were sometimes useless. Friends cut my food and poured my tea. My daughters combed my hair, brushed my teeth, and helped me dress. And, to top it all off, I gained well over 100 pounds! My doctor informed me that the only way Christians could commit suicide without appearing to do so was to eat themselves to death. Without realizing it, that was exactly what I was trying to do!

By the time Don and I met in 1976 at an Episcopal Renewal Conference in Kentucky, I weighed nearly 300 pounds and still had all my "itis's." It was at that conference I discovered forgiveness was the key to my spiritual, emotional and physical healing. Through prayer, the Holy Spirit ministered to me in pictures (Eph. 3:16) and took me back to my childhood around age four or five. He led me to my bedroom and sat on the bed with me. This was very significant since under that bed is where I spent much of my childhood hiding from my mother. With glaring eyes and gritted teeth she often threatened to cut me up in little pieces for stew meat. She would also shake me violently and throw me on the bed from across the room, shouting, "I hate you!"

Jesus put me on His lap and pulled me tightly into His chest, rocking me. He then took my face in His hands and looked at me with eyes full of such incredible love and comfort that I could never describe the peace, acceptance and unconditional love that flowed through my entire being. I was basking in His love for me and the joy He seemed to be feeling by just being there with me. My joy was beyond words – just being with Him was so comforting and incredible!!

Suddenly my mother appeared in the doorway. I tightened with fear. Jesus hugged me and assured me I was safe with Him. He picked me up off His lap and stood between my mother and myself. I felt totally protected. I'll never forget the words He spoke to her. He called her by name and said, "If you are going to cut anyone up for stew meat, cut me." Those words still ring in my mind today, for that is exactly what He did for each and every one of us when His flesh was cut and torn by flogging and His wrists and feet were pierced with nails as he hung on the cross dying for our sake.

Jesus returned to my bed and once again held me on His lap. He said to me, "Now you must forgive her." He helped me. Then He reminded me there was something for which I needed to be forgiven. I used to rub my mother's toothbrush on the bathroom floor. I also used it to clean a well-known fixture in the bathroom – sometimes referred to as the "church seat." In my young mind, I reasoned that if I could just get enough germs on her toothbrush, she might die before she could kill me by cutting me up in little pieces. Jesus forgave me and helped me forgive myself.

The spiritual healing that took place that evening was just the beginning. The next day as I was praying for someone to receive the baptism of the Holy Spirit, Jesus completely healed the arthritis, bursitis and tendinitis in my body. I suddenly had full range of motion and was totally without pain. It was an incredible witness to those attending the conference of God's continued miracles of healing today.

My friends from Michigan, Hank and Sally Murray and Tish Sanders with whom I attended also became good friends with Don. Throughout the following year, all of us, including Don, attended many other conferences together and our friendship grew. Nearly a year later, Don called me from his apartment in Kentucky and closed our conversation by saying, "I love you." I replied, "I love you, too," thinking he was referring to our loving fellowship in Christ. Sensing this, he called me back and said, "Anne, I'm IN love with you." My reaction was not good. When we hung up, I was very disappointed! I feared this would ruin our perfectly wonderful friendship. I thought of Don as a brother in the Lord, only, and that's the way I wanted it to remain. I had no intention of ever again getting involved in a romantic relationship. However, in the months that followed, God softened my heart and made it completely clear that He had chosen us for one another both in marriage and in ministry. I am absolutely positive of this with every fiber of my being! This year, 2014, we will celebrate our 37th wedding anniversary.

I am amazed at how many of our friends in Michigan knew Don and I would be married before we did. There were others in Kentucky who knew, as well. The late Emily Gardner Neal, The Reverend Lou Hemmers and his wife, Joan, all sensed that marriage was in our future. How grateful I am that they never mentioned this to me. It would have scared me in the opposite direction immediately and I might never have experienced the incredible life I've lived with Don as my precious, beloved husband and my second best friend, after Jesus. When we minister to couples whose marriages are "on the rocks," I am so grateful to God that our marriage is firmly established on "THE ROCK!!!!"

I now believe with all my heart that ours was a marriage pre-arranged in heaven without either of us knowing. Neither of us planned, nor did we desire, to ever marry again. In spite of us, Christ was working in the center of our very different lives.

God groomed us for this ministry to you. We love one another unconditionally and forever, just as He loves all of us. Jesus called on His disciples to go out two by two to heal the sick, bind the broken-hearted and set the captives free. (Mark 6:7). I am so blessed, grateful and honored that God chose Don to be my husband and my two-by-two partner with Him in ministry. Many couples have assured us how meaningful it is that we minister to them as a couple.

As a child of divorce, I have always yearned for the parental warmth and love that I missed. Don and I found ourselves in Oregon a few years ago at the bedside of my dying father who, at 92, had never accepted Jesus Christ into his life. For hours, Dad and I talked of those brief happy moments in my childhood when he taught me to ride a horse before I could walk. I thanked him for introducing me to the wonderful world of horses – animals that gave me unconditional love when no one else would. I thanked him for teaching me to swim, play tennis and golf. Then, pointing to the short time we'd spent together on this earth, I pleaded with Dad to accept Jesus as his Lord and Savior so that we could spend eternity together. He agreed, and my beloved Don led my beloved father to our Beloved Heavenly Father. Dad died the next morning. How awesome it is to know that my earthly father is with my heavenly Father today and that he loves me in a whole new way. Now, we will spend eternity together in the peace, joy, grace, and unconditional love of God.

I prayed fervently to God to give me the ability to love my mother with His love when we were invited by my daughter Anne to spend time as a family at Sun River Resort in Oregon. He so answered that prayer! Through forgiveness on both our parts, my mother and I now enjoy a reconciled relationship. To celebrate Mother's 100th birthday we are returning to Sun River this June. Our family will consist of: daughter Anne, her husband Bob, and their children Grace & Henry; daughter Bunni, her husband John, their daughters Megan & Lindsey and Lindsey's daughter Natalie. Unfortunately Bunni's daughter Maddie and her little boy Madden are unable to attend. We will be five generations. Wow! Tragedy has turned to treasure and my heart sings with joy! It never ceases to amaze me what God has in store for us if we will just have faith in Him, be obedient to His word and trust Him completely!

His everlasting peace is His gift to us as we bask in His presence on our life's journey with Him... the journey HE has chosen for us. And, oh, how I look forward to that journey!!

✤ Don's Story:

I am a Messianic Jew and a born again Christian. I grew up loving God. My family attended temple. I remember my mother lighting the Sabbath candles on Friday night and my father pronouncing blessings on our family. My Old Testament background has given me a deeper insight into the world of my Lord Jesus Christ. The old and new traditions are united within me. Becoming a Christian is not an easy journey. Conflict and cost came into play in my conversion, as my first marriage shattered in divorce and all family relationships suffered. God had a plan for my life. Today, I am blessed beyond description because I listened to Him.

I was 40 years old when I met my Yeshua - my Messiah. I remember learning about Him in the temple as one of the "good guy prophets of old." I also vividly remember learning to run swiftly in my mixed St. Louis neighborhood when bullies would chase me and try to beat me up for being a "Christ Killer," but I had never truly met Jesus until May 11, 1969.

At that time, I was a hard-working family man with a wife and three children. I had all the trappings of success, but felt a spiritual void in my life. My restlessness finally led me to accept an invitation to a weekend workshop at a local Episcopal Church. I came home that Sunday afternoon in May exhausted and confused. I flopped down, totally wiped out physically, emotionally and spiritually.

Sunday Night at the Movies, "Zorba the Greek," was playing on television, but I was dazed, drifting mentally into a favorite childhood pass-time that always calmed my nerves – working a jigsaw puzzle. Eventually, fixing my fuzzy gaze on the TV screen, my imaginary jigsaw puzzle pieces began falling into place. As Zorba's life unfolded, my life also unfolded.

After each tragedy in Zorba's life, he picked himself up and danced! He celebrated the life God had given him, regardless of his circumstances. At one time, he said to the Englishman, "When God gives you a gift, grab it!" Suddenly, the last piece of the puzzle fell into place. It was the face of Jesus and He was smiling at me!

7

Looking back at my first 40 years on this earth, I'm reminded of my Hebrew ancestors who wandered in the desert for 40 years searching for the Promised Land. On that Sunday afternoon in 1969, I found it! God gave me the gift of His Son that day and I grabbed it. Like Zorba, I've picked myself up and danced in the face of adversity ever since.

Many years later, back stage, Anne and I met Anthony Quinn, who played Zorba in both the movie and stage production. He shared that he was also spiritually touched by Zorba. I told Anthony Quinn that God the Father created me to dance; God the Son gave me permission to dance; God the Holy Spirit, through Zorba, taught me to dance. This statement was followed by a huge bear hug by Mr. Quinn. He said, over and over, "God Bless you, my son." He started crying and soon, his secretary, Anne and myself all stood in his dressing room weeping and hugging each other. It was a beautiful shared moment in the Lord and remains among our cherished memories.

Anne and I share many memories of our life together since we first met at that healing conference in 1976 sponsored by Episcopal Renewal Ministries. We had little in common when we first met except our faith in Christ. We came from totally different backgrounds – even different states. I lived in Kentucky and Anne lived in Michigan. I was going through a divorce. Anne was widowed. Marriage, or even a relationship beyond friendship, was the last thing on our minds. We had both been there, done that – thank you very much!

Our love was born with Christ in the center. When we fell in love a year later, began our marriage and then our ministry together, the pieces of a beautiful new puzzle began to form. Sailing the seven C's together for nearly 38 years, we've ministered through Jesus to hundreds of hurting couples. This book represents another piece of the puzzle. It is a piece that puts you and your spouse in a Christ-centered ship that does not sink, but dances joyfully on the rippling waves – just as Zorba danced joyfully on the shore so many years ago.

The Wedding Homily

SAIL THE SEVEN C'S OF MATRIMONY

1. COVENANT

A covenant is of the utmost importance to God. As you declare your marriage vows, you are making a covenant for your relationship to one another and to God. In Biblical times, covenants were made by blood sacrifices, the giving of robes and the giving of rings. In covenant with you, Jesus Christ willingly made a blood scrifice by giving up His life to save yours!

2. COMMITMENT

Today you are making a serious commitment to one another and to God in front of your family and friends. There is a mystery to becoming "Mr. and Mrs." This mystery is referred to in Genesis 2:24: *For this reason a man will leave his father and mother and be united to his wife, and the two shall become one flesh.* Through the commitment of marriage, two distinct individuals with different personalities, different backgrounds and different identities become ONE! Diversity remains! Unity reigns!

3. COMPASSION

This is the compassion of unconditional love! You are called to be compassionate companions. You are called to remember the scripture found in Romans 8:1, *There is no condemnation to those who are in Christ Jesus.* There is to be no condemnation of one another. As a compassionate companion to the one you love, ask yourself, "What would Jesus do or say in this situation?" Respond with His unconditional love for you and for your spouse!

4. COMMUNICATION

This speaks for itself. Pardon the pun! Without verbal communication, you will need to be mind readers, yet some couples expect their spouse to do just that – read their mind concerning their thoughts and feelings. Words are only 15% of communication. Body language and tone of voice are 85%. Verbally, share your thoughts and feelings. They are valid. Do this without blaming one another. Compromise is an important feature of communication. Every problem or potential problem has a solution that can be obtained through compromise. This can also be called negotiation. As spouses, you will need the skills of labor negotiators. Problems are never the problem: the problem arises through the way we learn to handle our issues. This is usually learned through the ways we witnessed our parents or significant others handle their problems. Someone once said, "Happiness is not the absence of conflict, but the ability to cope with it." Through sincere, verbal communication, willingness to compromise, and positive body language you can calm the waters and sail safely on together.

5. CONFLICT

Conflict is unavoidable. Far from being a negative concept, conflict is often the steppingstone to better understanding in a relationship. It has been said that pain is inevitable ... misery is optional. In Michele Weiner Davis' book, *The Divorce Remedy*, she states that it is a myth that conflict and anger are signs of a failing marriage. "People in loving marriages understand that conflict goes with the marital territory. It's more than unavoidable, it is necessary ... The fact is, the single best predictor of divorce is the constant avoidance of conflict!" Although few people enjoy confrontation and most would prefer to avoid it, conflict is inevitable. How you resolve it in your marriage is what is important. (Later in the book, we will include our "0-10" method of making decisions – a very helpful tool).

6. COST

There is indeed a cost for a long lasting, healthy marriage! The cost is giving up the right to be right. This is where you see the dark clouds above and know there are "storm warnings ahead." There IS a cost for forgiveness and repentance. The words, "I'm sorry" and "Please forgive me," are the beginning of forgiveness and need to be followed by repentance, which says, "I am turning away from whatever it was that hurt you." (A recent newspaper article claims that the two most difficult things for a man to say are "I need directions," and "I'm sorry.") You are called to give up your control of one another and to give control of your life to Jesus Christ in your marriage. Giving up control is a challenge. This is even more difficult than giving up the controls of the TV set! When you confess that "I do not have the permission or the right to control another human being," and you give up the right to be right, you die to self. Let go and let Christ lead the way. With Him at the helm, the cost is paid in full.

7. CELEBRATION!

Jesus knew how to celebrate! Isn't it interesting that His first recorded miracle happened at a wedding in Cana? Sharing laughter and hugs with the people you love is even healthier than the legendary apple a day. Laughter is contagious and hugs are healing. What joyous celebrations do you remember? Your first day of school, birthdays, holidays, graduations, weddings, anniversaries? It is God's plan that ALL of life is to be a celebration of His love for you! Celebrate every day! Even death is the final celebration of life on earth and our first incredible celebration of new life at the Father's banquet table. As you choose to celebrate your wedding day with joy and love, you can also choose to celebrate the days of your life in the same way. Rejoice in the Lord always! Again, I say Rejoice! Set sail on the Seven C's of marriage and celebrate the gift of one another every day of the exciting voyage ahead!

All Seven C's flow into, out of, around and through ONE HUGE C: CHRIST
Christ is the center, the Captain, Ship's Doctor, Navigator and the Compass, who blesses our Covenant, strengthens our Commitment, feels our Compassion, hears our Communication, pays our Cost, teaches us through Conflict, and rejoices in our Celebration!

NOTE:

Dietrich Bonhoeffer was a Lutheran Pastor in Germany when World War II broke out. He opposed Hitler, and even participated in an unsuccessful plot to assassinate him. Like Christ, Bonhoeffer chose to give up his life for others, when he could have remained safely in the United States. He was imprisoned and martyred for his belief. While in prison awaiting his execution, Bonhoeffer wrote a sermon to be read at his niece's wedding. Our entire message to you this day can be summed up with the following quote from his sermon:

> *"God gives you Christ as the foundation of your marriage. Welcome one another, therefore, as Christ has welcomed you, for the glory of God. In a word, live together in forgiveness, for without it no human fellowship, least of all a marriage, can survive. Don't insist on your rights, don't blame one another, don't judge or condemn one another, don't find fault with one another, but ACCEPT one another as you are, and forgive one another every day from the bottom of your hearts."* *

Here is your First Class Ticket to Sail the Seven C's! Marriages may be made in heaven, but the maintenance is here in the midst of the storm. We pray huge waves do not await you. However, if they do, take Jesus with you to calm the waters and keep you on course.

"Bon Voyage!"

* Reprinted with permission of Scribner, an import of Simon & Schuster Adult Publishing group from *Letters and Papers From Prison* by Dietrich Bonhoeffer. Copyright © 1953, 1967, 1971 by SCM Press Ltd.

Covenant

You have made a Covenant before your God,
your friends and your family.
This is extremely serious to God!
This is serious business to Satan, also.
Satan hates the Covenant of Marriage!
He is out to destroy it.

Covenant

Chapter One

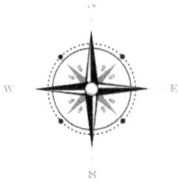

Covenant

Eternal Covenant

Joan and Bill met in church. *"Our families were thrilled when we decided to get married"* remembers Joan. *"Bill was a rising star in the banking business, and I thought we shared the same beliefs and goals. It seemed like our marriage was made in heaven. After all, both of us had gone to the right schools and had the right credentials. Bill was the young man you wanted to take home to meet your parents."*

Soon after they vowed to love one another for better or for worse, for richer or for poorer, through sickness and in health, and to cherish one another forever, Joan discovered that Bill was an alcoholic. *"Bill was a Type A personality – organized and purpose driven. In fact, that was one of the reasons I married him. I needed his organizational skills and the order and focus he brought to any situation. I wanted the travel and exciting lifestyle—the trappings that went along with his executive position."*

On the surface, Joan and Bill were the perfect couple; everyone reminded Joan how fortunate she was to have such a handsome, successful husband. But, behind closed doors, their life was far less than perfect. Combined with the alcohol, Bill's Type A personality had the power to crush Joan. He would spend the day aggressively pursuing his career at the bank, and then take out his frustrations on Joan after hours. *"Bill was so verbally abusive that it was frightening. It didn't take long before I began desperately searching for a way out of this disaster."*

While in college, Joan had been attracted to New Age materials and had become entwined in the occult, looking to horoscopes, tarot cards and other *"hidden knowledge"* sources seeking a deeper walk with the Lord (in the wrong places). She had even tried the cults, Christian Science and Unity—deceived into thinking that she was still following the Lord Jesus Christ. Being in this deception could not help her out of the situation she was now facing in her marriage. But, God had a plan....

When Joan's dad became seriously ill, she attended a Kathryn Kuhlman healing service with her parents. "My parents were devoted Christians and had no idea what I'd been doing with my spiritual life," she admits. "I went to the service for my dad and ended up meeting my Heavenly Father. All of my questioning and seeking answers elsewhere collapsed like a house of cards. Kathryn Kuhlman gave an altar call and I responded. Although I'd been in Church all my life, I suddenly found myself 'born again' and every childhood Bible verse and story, every liturgy passage, every choir song came back to me vividly in night visions. When I came back from the service, Bill looked at me as if I'd gone off the deep end and said, 'You are reading that Bible as if your life depended on it.' I was, and my life did depend on it!"

Immediately, Joan began attending a spirit-filled Episcopal Church again on a regular basis and she asked her pastor to help her seek the Lord's guidance for her troubled marriage. She prayed that the Lord would grant her a way out of the Covenant that she had made on her wedding day. She was sure that the Lord would agree with her since neither she nor Bill knew the meaning of Covenant when they had spoken those words.

One morning as she was making the bed, she heard God's voice. "It wasn't like words. It was like a rippling stream—so gentle, so loving, and so powerful. He said... 'I do not want you to seek a divorce from your husband. You made a Covenant with Me as well as with him. If you will allow Me, I will give you the grace to keep your Covenant vows to Me—in My Strength.'" After that day, Joan knew that she would be given the grace to stay, not because she loved Bill, but because she loved God. She learned to love Bill through God's eyes as she walked in her gifting as an intercessor, praying for others as well as for Bill, herself and their marriage.

As an intercessory prayer leader, God gave Joan the gift to see people as He sees them. "It sounds strange, but when He asks me to pray for people, He shows me what they look like to Him." Joan had always aspired to be a registered nurse and enjoyed visiting people in the *hospital as part of her ministry. One place in the hospital that she always managed to avoid was the burn ward. "I couldn't stand to see the pain there. Then one day God showed me Bill as He saw him—a burn victim, hurting and angry from all the deep inner wounds of his past. Even to touch him with healing ointment would cause excruciating pain. Seeing him like that gave me the compassion I needed to stay by his side, no matter what."*

Even when things are not easy, the Lord is faithful. At 30, Joan discovered that they were destined to be childless. It was a devastating blow to a woman who needed so desperately to give and receive love. Soon after that, Bill's father left his mother and they became responsible emotionally and financially for his mother and sixteen-year-old sister. Bill's older sister's marriage with two young children also fell apart around the same time. Bill and Joan ministered support to them as well. Just at a time when Bill's earnings were supporting so many, that financial stability began to wane as he lost his job at the bank. He found other employment, but things were not the same.

In time, Bill and Joan moved to South Florida to manage the business that her parents had spent a lifetime building together—a successful business that was now in serious financial trouble. Within 8 years, the business was sold and the employees blamed Joan and Bill for its failure. It was the bottom that Bill needed to hit—it was the dark night of the soul for them both. "At that time, our Baptist pastor led Bill through the sinner's prayer and Bill gave his life to Christ. It was at that time as well that Bill sought help for his alcoholism and, with the Lord's grace, remains in sobriety to this day."

It was after Bill and Joan moved to Central Florida that they met Don and Anne Bloch. "Don and Anne would come to our Episcopal Church once a month (for several days at a time) to minister to our congregation and, as I was one of the intercessory prayer leaders, it was our privilege to have them stay at our home. Somehow, in spite of the big front we put on and the healing that we had experienced in our marriage, Don and Anne saw right through us. Although they never said it, they could see my buried unforgiveness toward Bill and Bill's continued anger at life in general. It was wonderful how they ministered to us and prayed for us in such a gentle, loving way—especially through their beautiful example. The masks we were wearing began to fall away in their wonderful presence. Like Jesus, they pressed out the unforgiveness with the Love of the Lord. I was like a dry sponge soaking up water, and that poisonous water was the bitterness I still harbored in my heart toward Bill."

Joan and Bill's healing was not easy. Serious medical problems began plaguing Bill and, Joan would call Don and Anne to pray for Bill and for their marriage. Don and Anne would often visit and minister to them. Eventually, financial and medical problems caused them to sell their home and temporarily move to a small apartment. One night, Joan had a dream that she and Bill had lost everything and would never gain it back. It was something that she had feared more than anything else…Poverty! In going before the Lord with this terrifying concern, she again heard God's voice speaking to her, reassuring her that *"I have prepared a place for you and Bill."* Joan clung to that promise of Peace in the storm of life. As Joan looked at the man lying close to her, she realized that Bill and his family were now worshipping God with her. She realized that the misfortunes they had experienced together had strengthened their Covenant to one another and to God. She realized the most amazing thing of all. She was passionately in love with Bill. She was rich!

"After 35 plus years, we are still rich in sharing God's love. Bill prays with me and for me now. He has been in a continual healing process. We have a great church family. I am so very grateful that God did not allow me to break our marriage Covenant. On the worldly side, things still look a bit tentative sometimes; but, on the eternal side, we are tremendously blessed."

Quoting Psalm 91, Joan says, "A thousand may fall at your side, ten thousand at your right hand, but it will not come near you." Noting that the Psalm could apply to current divorce statistics and that she and Bill might have easily been among them had she not been obedient to the Lord's leading to keep their marriage Covenant, Joan sighs with relief. "He never guaranteed that Bill would come to salvation, but he has. He never guaranteed that I'd fall in love with my husband again, but I have. He never guaranteed that our families would come to such an intimate knowledge of Him, but they have. Now I know that we will be together with the Lord through eternity. Our God's faithful, awesome, Covenant loving-kindness is indeed better than life!"

Best Friends Forever

Diana loved Jim from the first moment she laid eyes on him in 6ᵗʰ grade. "He's been my best friend forever," says Diana, "Growing up, he was always there for me when I needed him." Diana and Jim attended different high schools and colleges, but remained close. By the time they began dating in college, each of them had experienced serious emotional and spiritual set-backs. Diana was a victim of alcohol-related date rape and one of her dearest college friends died in an automobile accident. Jim had been heavily involved in the partying scene at his college. They were both at a point in their lives when they needed someone they could trust – and who better than their best friend?

After six years of dating, they finally married. "We were 28 when we got married and 30 when we had our first daughter, but we were still partners, constantly seeking new thrills. Even though we'd been raised in Christian homes, we were not in a good spiritual place." When Jim admitted, following a marriage builders weekend, that he struggled with lust, his admission rocked Diana's world, causing her to face her own serious insecurities and doubts.

Jim and Diana had been married nearly seven years when they attended Don and Anne's "Marriage on the Rock" class and knew they needed help. "The intimacy was lost in our relationship," Diana says. "I knew I loved Jim, but I didn't want him to touch me and I didn't know why." Seeking the ministry of Don and Anne, they began to see how the carnage of past sins and secrets was eating away at their marriage.

"The enemy has strongholds on our lives that can be fairly subtle and he uses those over time to destroy marriage," says Jim, using the analogy of the cat burglar who comes in the night and steals a few pieces of silver; the next night, a lamp; and the next night, some jewelry. Night after night, the thief returns to take a bit here and a bit there until one morning you wake up in an empty house. "A turning point for us was when we broke through the secrecy in our lives and allowed ourselves to become vulnerable. Things in our past weren't so great and we still held on to them. We needed Don and Anne to give us a safe place to reveal our secrets, to experience God's grace and forgiveness."

 With Jesus in the center, Jim and Diana now have an intimacy and trust in their marriage that was missing before. They are joyfully fulfilled and they love sharing that joy with other couples - especially troubled couples who are in need of the power of God's forgiveness in their lives. "All marriages are a work in progress," said Jim, "but without good Christian community pointing us back to the power of forgiveness, we might not have made it."

 Now secure in herself as a child of God and an adored wife, Diana has become a strong warrior woman for marriage. "Jim and I have fought for four other marriages because of what we've been through. We have begged God to help our friends, pouring encouragement into them. It's in the knowing that you get the help, and we know what God's love can do to heal a marriage."

 Seeking counsel and help from fellow Christians is, in Diana's view, a sign of strength, not weakness. "I wish people would know there's no quick fix. It's like peeling an onion. We go back to Don and Anne regularly for a checkup and we seek God's guidance every day. God placed this love in our hearts so long ago. Now, I see Jim and still get that flutter – he's still that boy I fell in love with in 6th grade."

Genesis 2:24
For this reason a man will leave his father and mother and be united with his wife, and they will become one flesh.

The covenant we make on our wedding day is based on the above scripture. We covenant to leave our parents and our past and become a new family. In no way does this dishonor our parents! It is to honor them for participating with God to bring us into the world, to give us love, acceptance, guidance and security to the best of their ability. Even when parents fail in giving us some of these qualities, we are still to honor them for giving us life. There has never been a perfect set of parents.

If we cannot leave our parents, physically, emotionally or spiritually, we will continue to be bogged down in the past. We cannot live in the present nor move into the future with our feet still planted in the past. Notice that God's very clear instructions are to leave parents before you cleave to one another. Leave - then cleave!

(Anne): I have always been fascinated with Don's Jewish Heritage. He has a marvelous way of explaining this from a Biblical perspective. Although it has no bearing on the customs of today, in ancient of days, the betrothal began with what we refer to as an engagement. The husband-to-be actually builds a home from scratch for his bride-to-be, while living with his father. This can sometimes take as long as a year. Since it is not known when the house will be finished, it is, therefore, not known when the groom will return for his betrothed. This is why the ten virgins were instructed to keep extra oil for their lamps, so they and the rest of the wedding guests could light the way to escort them to their new home, where the groom's father has prepared a wedding feast. *See Matthew 25:1-13 and John 14:1-4.* Likewise, we are instructed to be prepared for the day Jesus comes for us to take us to our new home in Heaven where we will share with Him the feast prepared by our Heavenly Father at His banquet table.

1 + 1 = 1

As we enter the 21st century, the Body of Christ needs a reminder that the marriage relationship is a reflection of our relationship with Jesus Christ. Those who discover the joy of their salvation have found that death to self is a necessary ingredient in Jesus coming alive in us. So it is in marriage. The two becoming one requires death to self. The unity candle that is lit during the ceremony is only validated when the bride and groom extinguish their individual candles. The two become one when they are willing to lay down their lives for one another and for God, love unconditionally and form a brand new union. 1 + 1 = 1!

Throughout the Old Testament, covenantal living was of utmost importance. After God created His universe, He declared it as good. After God created Adam, He declared that event as VERY good! However, God soon made a startling statement. It seemed that Adam had everything. He had an abundance of food, a place to rest, a perfect environment in The Garden of Eden and held the exalted position of having dominion over everything! With all that Adam had, God still made the statement, "It is NOT good for man to be alone." (Genesis 2:18) God created Eve to be Adam's partner and helpmate. She was an equal partner for Adam.

1 + 1 = 2

God then made the first of His 613 laws and commandments and instructed them "To be fruitful and multiply."

Today's culture, through Satan's influence, has God's plan reversed! Today, it has become socially acceptable to live together prior to marriage – even to have children together before saying the sacred vows. God calls us into the sacred covenant of marriage (called a sacrament in some churches) between a man and a woman — then to share a bed and bear children! Too often we hear the myth that God's Word is irrelevant today. We continue to get bogged down in the quicksand of self-centeredness and instant gratification. God's plan was, is and will forever be the marriage covenant first, then to live together, and then to become good stewards of His gift of children if that is His plan for you.

God's Covenants

God made a covenant with Noah after the flood, and used the rainbow as the sign of this covenant that never again would a flood destroy the earth. He made a significant everlasting covenant with Abraham. Covenants can be found throughout the Old Testament. It is not our intent to teach on each covenant God has made. It is our desire to focus upon the most important Blood Covenant God has made on behalf of His people. Our most gracious and merciful God knew his people were heading for disaster. He sent His Son to us as a redeeming sacrifice and a sign of The New Covenant, as prophesied by numerous Old Testament prophets. At the Last Supper, as Jesus was celebrating the Seder Passover Meal, He declared that His shed blood would be a NEW covenant for us. By The Cup and The Matzo (unleavened bread) we have been redeemed and reconciled back to God The Father because Jesus took upon Himself all our sins.

Sacrificial Love

For those who take seriously the covenant of marriage and the sacrificial love of Jesus, the blessings will flow from God beyond measure. We are also called upon to manifest sacrificial love to our spouse... even the sacrificial love of giving our lives for our spouse just as Christ gave His life for us.

Many times the Middle Eastern custom of a covenant was sealed with blood. There was also a custom of the giving of a robe, which is how David and Jonathan made a covenant with one another. Giving something was a sign of a covenant, be it a robe, blood, ring or other prized possession. This conveys that, "All I have is yours and all that I am is yours."

Covenant or Contract?

According to Craig Hill, author of the book, *Marriage*: *Covenant or Contract*, "The concept of a covenant, then, is a unilateral, irrevocable commitment valid at least to death. Covenant does not depend on performance of either party." On the other hand, "A contract is a bilateral agreement between two parties totally dependent upon performance of the agreement." Contracts have conditions to be met. If not met, a contract may be broken. Contracts may have a warranty involved. A covenant does not. Warranties are based on performance, covenants are not.

In today's Western culture, the marriage covenant has become more like a marriage contract that says, "As long as I'm happy I will stay in this relationship." Regrettably, the church in general has bought into this destructive and seductive behavior. However, more and more churches are turning away from the concept of being "wedding factories." About 75% of all weddings are officiated by the church. This presents a great opportunity for the Body of Christ to return to God's original covenant principles. We suggest you read *Marriage Savers* by Michael J. McManus to learn of more opportunities for the church to save marriages.

Years ago, we met an extraordinary couple at a conference where we were the speakers in the Cincinnati, Ohio area. Louise and Maurice Mandel's voices were a gift from God as they led us in worship. One duet they sang has stuck with us for thirty plus years. It is a song of THE marriage covenant to which we are to hold fast. It would be awesome if this were sung at every wedding! The song is *All That I Am,** written by Sebastian Temple. The words are as follows:

> All that I am …
> All that I do …
> All that I'll ever have …
> I offer now to you.
> Take and sanctify these gifts for your honor, Lord
> Knowing that I love and serve you …… is enough reward.
> All that I dream …
> All that I pray …
> And all that I'll ever make …
> I give to you this day.

(Don): Remember that story when God mentioned the topic of baseball in His book? "In the big inning..." Seriously, in the beginning, God created the universe. His plan has always been to be a relational God. It was always His desire that there be a "vertical" relationship between man and Himself. When God created Eve to be Adam's helpmate, the horizontal relationship between a husband and a wife came into existence. The vertical relationship was one of sacrificial love. The horizontal relationship, also, was meant to be sacrificial, but, regrettably, the sacrificial aspect of marriage is often neglected. When a marriage covenant is established in sacrificial love, it can weather any storm at sea. If the covenant is broken, the human suffering is excruciating.

I know this, because I come to you as a man who broke the sacred marriage covenant by divorcing my first wife. My divorce caused much pain and grief. I am certain that it grieved God's heart as well.

Since that time, I have learned much about God's forgiveness of my sins. Through many prayers to my Heavenly Father for forgiveness and my repentance, I have personally experienced God's awesome grace. The gift of His grace is a precious one that none of us deserve. I guess that is why we call it "grace."

Divorce – The Devil's Tool

Today's headlines are full of the toll that divorce is taking on society. Single parent homes are the norm rather than the exception. Statistics have shown that our society is currently made up of 1/3 single-parent homes, 1/3 step-family homes and only 1/3 of the homes represent the traditional family that God intended when He created Adam and Eve. Across America and across the world, leaders are encouraging marriage covenants that are meaningful as a way to stem the tide of social disintegration. Your marriage is precious in God's eyes and in the eyes of your family, and friends. It is imperative that your marriage be precious to you!

Do you understand that you are presently in the midst of a spiritual battle with Satan when your marriage covenant is threatened? Your mind is the battlefield. When you put Christ in the center of your marriage at the altar, the devil immediately begins circling – looking for kinks in your armor – cracks in your covenant. He wants to break into that center and replace love with discontent. The war is raging in the midst of your joyous union and you are in the thick of the battle.

In our years of ministry, we have met couples who have actually succumbed to satanic worship. It is more common than you can imagine. As we ministered with these couples, it was *only* through the grace of our Lord Jesus Christ that we were able to help them. They have given us detailed descriptions of monthly satanic services where blood sacrifices were made and prayers were chanted against Christian marriages – especially those of clergy, or anyone in church leadership.

Satan loves it when the Covenant of Marriage is broken. Unfortunately, he's had a lot to smile about lately. Without Christ in your marriage, you are fighting a fearful enemy with a water pistol. Defeat is inevitable. Your ship is sinking.

Fill your water pistols with God's living water. Wipe that smile off Satan's face!

(Anne): It was only when Jesus came to live in my heart that I realized the seriousness of all God's covenants. Then I was guilt-ridden all over again; this time not only because I had hurt my two daughters whom I adore, also because I had hurt the heart of my Lord, who I also adore.

ONLY through learning of God's grace, mercy, unconditional love and the fact that Jesus died on the cross so our sins can be forgiven has my heart been healed. It's as if I spent the years of my first two marriages water-skiing through life – merely skimming the surface. Since accepting Jesus into my heart, I have escaped the turbulent seas of unforgiveness and become an accomplished 'scuba diver' in His living waters.

My guilt and shame have been forgiven and I have been washed clean as freshly fallen snow. My regret and hopelessness have been turned into hope, my spirit renewed, my life transformed. God indeed has turned my mourning into dancing!

At the wedding of my daughter, Anne, for which the Seven C's were given to Don, I asked my former husband to please forgive me for any hurt I had caused him and for not fighting for our marriage. He forgave me, although he has never asked my forgiveness for his affairs during our marriage. That is between him and God. My beloved daughters, Anne and Bunni, have also graciously forgiven me for the hurts I have caused them. Praise and glory to my precious Daddy God! Through His forgiveness I have been set free and filled with His living water…the only water in which you can breathe…the only water that brings true peace, joy, happiness and contentment. He has made me righteous in His sight so that I can have an everlasting, personal relationship with Him. Alleluia! It makes me want to dance in The Spirit!

I truly believe God has used the incredible pain of my divorce to help you avoid the same agony. If you are contemplating divorce, I implore you to allow me to share with you what I wish someone had told me many years ago.

If you have children, you will be sharing them with another man or woman and their entire family when your spouse remarries. Nothing hurts quite so much as hearing your child say to their stepparent on the phone, in your presence, "I love you and miss you." In retrospect, I now am grateful for their loving relationship with their step-mother. However, this personal heartache of being forced to share children and grandchildren is one that perpetuates itself for generations to come.

When I became a single parent, my oldest daughter, Bunni, was a toddler and my youngest, Anne, still an infant. Those were the hardest, saddest, loneliest, most agonizing years of my life. It was absolutely devastating every Christmas, Easter and summer when I packed their suitcases to be with their father and stepmother for their entire vacation. I had them for the every day grind of discipline and training – they had them for the special times. They had them for the fun of life…I had them for the facts of life. It tore my heart out every time I put them on an airplane for those many years. I missed my girls more than words can describe. There was a constant, aching hole in my heart when they were gone. I missed out on so much of their lives. You will too! Please, oh, please learn from my mistakes. In not forgiving you are breaking your coventant with God, your spouse, and even your children. The cost of unforgiveness is much too high a price to pay…for everyone involved! You will sink into the deep waters of dispair, bitterness, loneliness, and a broken heart.

COVENANT
Ponder Page ...

1. How will you celebrate your covenant with God and one another on your next anniversary?

2. Ephesians 5:31: *For this reason a man will leave his father and mother and be united with his wife and the two will become one flesh.* Is there anything in the relationship with your parents that is standing in the way of the two of you becoming one flesh?

3. Is there anything or anyone you need to leave behind for the sake of your relationship?

4. Is there anything within you that is blocking your coventant, be it hurt, unconfessed sin or unforgiveness?

5. Is there anything you need to change for the sake of your relationship?

6. Discuss with your spouse the importance of covenant vs contract in your marriage.

Commitment

Make the commitment to be joyous together
in body, mind and spirit.
Love one another with compassion and commitment
that comes from your heart.
Allow Christ to reside in your heart.
When you bless one another daily,
it is like a morning kiss from Christ!
What a lovely way to start the day!

Commitment

Chapter Two

Commitment

Committing a "Legg's Egg" to Christ

John and Susan celebrated their 35th wedding anniversary recently, but it was in 1979 that their true marriage really began.

"I went to a men's retreat and Don Bloch was the leader," remembers John. "God spoke to my heart that weekend and I experienced emotional healing. I walked into the house and told Susan I loved her totally for the first time. It was the beginning of new life in our dying marriage."

John and Susan came from very different backgrounds.

John grew up on a farm. His father was disabled and, as a result, John carried heavy responsibilities on his shoulders from a very young age. At 13, he was driving a tractor and virtually running the farm that supported his family. They went to church every Sunday and lived a simple, disciplined life on the farm. After graduating from college, John was determined to have all the material things he never had as a child. He drove himself to succeed and rose to the top in his profession.

Susan grew up in the city with an alcoholic father, an invalid mother and abusive brothers. Her family sneered at God and people who believed in Him. By the time she married John, she had been sexually abused for years and was a young woman with low morals and even lower self-esteem.

"I was a virgin when we married," says John. "We had great sex and a well-stocked liquor cabinet that Susan made good use of. Susan had no concept of money. She was wasteful and careless, no matter how much I earned. I focused on my job where everything was under my control, because I felt I had no control at home. No matter how bad things got in our marriage, I was raised in a family that believed marriage was a sacred covenant. There were no divorces in my family, so I was committed to spend my life with this woman, but I let her know that she *didn't deserve it. When I came home to a dirty house and a burned dinner, I would go crazy, ranting and raving. The kids would fade into their rooms and shut the door. Our home-life was hell."*

"I really tried to be a good wife," says Susan, "but I felt like I never got any help. The more John criticized, the worse things got. He took our only car to work and I felt trapped at home with the kids all day. Money was a major issue. John was very controlling and hated to part with cash. He was so nice to the people at work and so mean to his family. It seemed like there was always anger boiling up inside him – just waiting to explode. Anything could set him off. Sometimes he would push me into the wall and put his hands around my throat. When he was mad, which was nearly all the time, he would throw the past up to me. I lived in constant fear."

When John came home from the retreat with new love in his heart, Susan had her doubts. She had recently been attending a bible study, getting rides from her neighbor, and was beginning to accept Jesus as her savior, but she felt that she was unworthy and beyond forgiveness for the things she had done in her past.

John convinced her to attend a weekend marriage encounter and, again, he ran into Don Bloch. This time, Anne Bloch was there, too, and offered her help to Susan. "John wanted to get our marriage "fixed," remembers Susan. "But I was afraid of Anne. I couldn't let her find out about the real me."

During the first few prayer and ministry sessions they had with John and Susan, Don and Anne zeroed in on John and his temper, with prayers for inner healing.

NOTE: There are many stories throughout the scriptures of God's healing of physical ailments. God also heals our emotions – part of the inner make-up of our soul. Jesus Christ is the same "yesterday, today and tomorrow" (Hebrews 13:8). He will not invalidate past hurts to our soul, but He CAN and WILL remove the sting of those hurts. This is referred to as "inner healing." (Eph. 3:16)

It was during this ministry with John that the Holy Spirit revealed the root of his anger. Many times in John's teenage years, he had come home after school to do the chores at his family's dairy farm when he preferred to be at school playing football or hanging out with his peers. He was still angry with his dad about the heavy burdens of responsibility placed on him. However, in spite of his deep anger, the boy had felt a commitment to his family, knowing they could not afford to hire extra help. By the time he became an adult, the anger was deeply buried, erupting in violent, unreasonable bouts of temper.

Don and Anne invited the Holy Spirit to reveal to John a vision in his mind of a safe, comfortable place he enjoyed as a child.

NOTE: This is NOT guided imagery! Guided imagery is a human-directed situation when a counselor tells the client what they should be seeing in their imagination. This can be extremely manipulative and dangerous. With inner healing, ONLY the Holy Spirit gives the person a vision if He so desires. In no way is this manipulation.

John saw himself lying in a cow pasture on a warm, sunny day looking up at the beautiful sky. It was a soothing picture for him. He recalled doing this often – just daydreaming. As this God-given picture was revealed to him, John noticed that he was lying next to a cow, with his head resting on the cow's soft udder. How caring of God to use the very animal John had detested as a youth to set him free!

An inner voice spoke to John, telling him how thankful and proud God was of him for the sacrifices he'd made for his family when they could not have survived without him. As John saw himself forgiving his dad and receiving affirmation and forgiveness from God, the deep-seated resentment and anger he had held inside for so many years gently flowed from him. He was re-leased from the bondage of uncontrollable anger that day.

John and Susan continued to see Don and Anne regularly, and when a fire broke out on the roof of their home, John decided to stay home the following morning and work on the roof, urging Susan to keep a scheduled appointment with the Blochs. Don was also unable to be there that day, leaving Anne and Susan alone for the first time. "Anne and I took a long ride together. We ended up in a church about 25 miles from home. We entered the empty church. Anne held my hands and began to pray."

Anne and Susan prayed together for the guidance of the Holy Spirit. Returning to her childhood, Susan saw Jesus standing behind the uncle who had abused her. She suddenly felt the forgiveness of Jesus in her heart for that uncle. She saw her brother who had raped her when she was 12 years old. She saw Jesus forgiving him. She saw her parents discussing an abortion and realized they were talking about aborting her – the ultimate rejection! She saw her children and the hurt in their eyes when she drank. She saw John and the multitude of men she'd known before him. She and Anne prayed together in the empty church from 10 a.m. until 7 p.m.

"My visions of the past were vivid. Through them all, Jesus kept coming back again and again and forgiving everyone who had hurt me. Always, his eyes were full of forgiveness for me, too," says Susan. "Anne asked me to gift-wrap all the people I'd forgiven and present them to Jesus. My last vision was of a huge Legg's Egg [a bright pink egg-shaped pantyhose container] with a big bow on it that was full of all my garbage. In my mind, I placed that egg full of trash at the foot of the cross. I was reborn that day – like a brand new baby chick emerging from an egg."

It was late and they were 25 miles from home, but Anne knew it was miracle time. She called John and said, "God wants you here. Susan needs you here. Get here!" Don came to the church with John. They called the Episcopal Priest, who arrived and began to prepare the Eucharist. "Don covered me in prayer on the way to that church," says John. "He went in first. When I entered the church, I looked around and saw Anne, but no Susan. Then I noticed a tiny girl peeking out from behind Anne's skirt. She had curly hair and a huge smile on her little face. She was smiling at me! Suddenly, she was Susan. I heard a voice, saying, "Ask Susan who she is. Tell her you love her and ask her to marry you." With the communion in the little church that night, John and Susan's spiritual divorce ended and they committed to live out their covenant with God.

John still loses his temper sometimes, and once in a while, Susan burns dinner or puts too much on the charge card. "Now, when we have an argument, we back off and start praying," says John. "Things go better when you pray together. Every morning, we bless one another and, when they're around, we bless our children, too, verbally and sincerely. We've made a commitment to love one another as God intended from the start." Susan has learned that marriage is a continual process and that regular renewal of their commitment to one another is necessary. "The difference is that now I know I'm loved by John and God. My commitment to keep Christ in the center of our marriage has set me free!"

Christ Emergency!

Tom and Sally had a loose, carefree lifestyle that many of their friends envied. They lived on a boat and both of them loved to party. Tom was making a ton of money traveling around the world heading up a company that did a type of marine repair that was his specialty. They had five children and their life was a loud, rollicking good time filled with fun and laughter. Or so it seemed. One day, Sally made the discovery that Tom was not a faithful husband. Suddenly, the laughter stopped.

"Sally was going to leave me," recalls Tom. "I knew, with our five kids, there was no way I could afford a divorce. I had really thought a lot of myself – like I was too big to fail, but now, it was time to straighten up and start living right. If there was any way I could save our marriage, I was determined to do it. Tom's father had been an alcoholic in the Navy and had put his mother through pure hell.

"No matter what, though, my mother had stayed with him and kept their marriage together. She wouldn't let our family fall apart because of troubles and I couldn't let that happen either. My mother would have been horrified at what I had done. She was a Christian woman who read her Bible religiously." Tom had always known that some day he'd become a Christian, but he knew that "some day" was now.

"It seems to me," muses Tom, "that the vast majority of people don't get down on their knees and seek Christ until it's an emergency, and I guess that's what happened to me!"

They had attended an Episcopal Church once in a while and Tom thought about talking with the Priest, but he knew the Priest had not been too impressed with their lifestyle, so when Tom's sister suggested they go see Don and Anne Bloch, and Sally said she'd go, they went.

When they first talked with Don and Anne, Tom was filled with remorse and more than ready to hand his life over to God. Sally loved Tom and wanted him to be a better husband and father. She knew she had some work to do on herself as well. They talked and listened and met with Don and Anne several times before coming to some major life-changing decisions.

Tom had been working out of town non-stop and that was one of the factors that had started the marriage going downhill. One of the decisions Don and Anne helped them make was that Tom would have to get rid of his successful company and his busy schedule in order to be at home with his family more regularly.

"I got rid of my employees and we rented a beach house and I went to work at the shipyards, and we ended up doing just as well financially with me at home," recalls Tom. "We started attending church regularly with all five kids. We had our own little circus. It was an event when we went to church, but we really began to bond as a family. God was central to our healing."

Tom called Don and Anne in 2013, some twenty years after he and Sally sought their ministry and made the decision to put Christ in the center of their marriage. "I just wanted to tell them that they glorify God and that without their guidance, we wouldn't have the wonderful marriage we have today," says Tom. "We're very happy. Our children are raised and we have many friends who are envious of our marriage. We've discovered that you can't find the full potential of your marriage without God. In fact, without God, you can't find the full potential of anything."

John 8:12
"I am the light of the world.
Whoever follows me will never live in darkness, but will have the light of life."

Do you remember the childhood riddle that asked, "What comes first, the chicken or the egg?" The question we raise here is what comes first, covenant or commitment? What are some of the differences between covenant and commitment? We suggest that the marriage covenant is what we are committing to uphold. We also commit ourselves to one another when we make our covenant with God.

When we say "I will," we are making a covenantal agreement with our will. This involves us emotionally and spiritually as well as physically. "I do" refers to the present time. "I will" is a commitment which includes the present and the future.

In making your commitment to your spouse, you also need to break soul ties from anyone in your past in order to be totally set free and committed to one another. This is accomplished through prayer, which eliminates carrying the heavy burden of past relationships into your marriage.

We can also use a vertical and horizontal visualization to give us a better understanding of commitment. Our covenant is a vertical connection to God. The commitment is the horizontal connection between husband and wife.

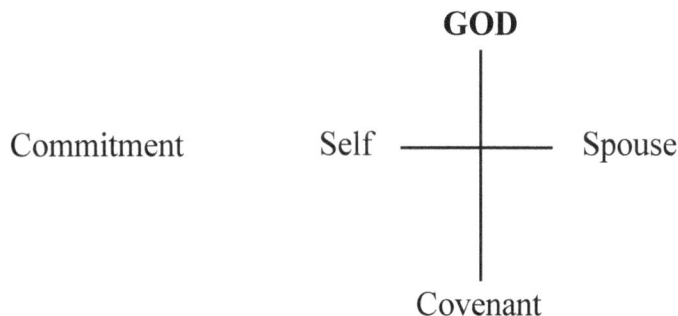

GOD

Commitment   Self ———+——— Spouse

Covenant

My Wife and I fight!

(Don): Fight? You are probably wondering "how strange to have this word in the C of Commitment!" It seems as if it would be in the "sea of conflict." Actually, it is there also!

My wife and I fight. Frankly we advise every couple coming to see us to prepare to fight. As Christian believers, they will be in a fight. It is a requirement for a husband and wife to fight – to fight daily! This is NOT an option…… The fighting may even intensify, and it is worthwhile. Make a commitment to fight daily. You will need to fight as a solid team effort and NOT one another.

Here's the scoop:

During the premarital or engagement stage of your relationship, there is great joy, happiness and infatuation. Upon returning from your honeymoon, reality and stress at work and home enters into the scene. As a Christian couple, you soon realize there is an unseen enemy lurking and "roaring like a lion looking for someone to devour." That is you! (I Peter 5:8-11.) Peter also gives a good antidote to "RESIST HIM - FIGHT BACK – STAND FIRM – KEEP UP YOUR GUARD – KEEP YOUR FAITH (in God) – PRAY FERVENTLY DAILY!"

It was explained earlier in this book how we learned that many Satanists will pray to Satan for the destruction of Christian marriages with an emphasis upon those in leadership roles. This is the reason a husband and wife have to fight back. Although the darts are aimed at you, God's promise is that with Him you have victory!

Do not go into the "woe is me or "woe are we" mode! Use these next few words to know you have already been given every tool to stop the onslaught of darts from the evil one! Your first task is to put on the armor of God EVERY morning. We know friends who visualize doing this very thing upon getting out of bed.

They actually see themselves putting on the belt of TRUTH around their waste followed by the breastplate of RIGHTEOUSNESS, the gospel of PEACE on their feet, picking up the shield of FAITH, the helmet of SALVATION and finally the sword of the HOLY SPIRIT. Now they are ready for battle! (Ephesians 6:10 – 18)

Husbands, you need to pray DAILY in the name of JESUS for the protection of your wife and children if and when you have them. Pray in the Spirit on all occasions and be alert. Likewise wives, you are to pray a blessing over your husbands for protection and guidance.

One of our favorite scriptures we claim every day for one another is John 10:10. *"The thief comes only to steal and kill and destroy (*including your marriage); *I (Jesus) have come that they* (husbands and wives) *may have life, and have it to the full."*

My wife, Anne and I fight daily – to stop any power or influence of the evil one in our marriage, family, home, church family, extended family, friends and ministry in the mighty name of Jesus! We highly recommend that you do the same.

Connecting with God

Let us be certain we first vertically connect with our God, receive His blessings, then horizontally join with one another as husband and wife. How do we connect with God? It is simple: through prayer, studying God's Word and ridding yourself of any unforgiveness.

If God's Word, the Bible, is unfamiliar, here is an incredible way to become aware of His plan for you. Before opening the Bible, pray for the Holy Spirit to give you the guidance you seek. Then read the verses as if they were love letters written to you. For instance, there was an executive some years ago who yearned to connect with God. He instructed his secretary to copy the letters from Paul in the New Testament verbatim, except that rather than being written to Corinthians or Philippians, the letters were directed to the executive. Each day, he received a letter from Paul. Each day, he became more connected with God.

To verbally connect with God, prayer is the answer. Prayer is a conversation between two persons in love. It is also through our love affair with Jesus that we connect with God. Compassionate conversation, vital in our love affair with our spouse, is just as vital in our communication with God. Prayer is both speaking to God AND listening to Him.

For most of us, listening is the missing part of our prayer life. Find a time and a place each day when you can speak to your Lord. Then be still. Listen for His gentle inner voice. It is alright if there is just silence at that time. Sometimes you will merely feel peace and contentment. At times, He may speak to you later in a dream, thought, or vision, through His scriptures or even through another person. We have experienced all of these methods of conversations with God. You probably have experienced some of them also, even if you didn't recognize them at the time.

(Anne): Many times I feel His presence and love so powerfully that I merely sit and cry, worshiping Him with praise and thanksgiving. Those moments bring such incredible peace and joy to my soul - peace and joy and hope that could ONLY come from HIM!

Blessings

Prayer time should end with a Blessing that the husband pronounces upon his wife and she upon him. If children are present, the Blessing should be pronounced upon each child as well. It is awesome for children to hear their own names spoken as you lay hands on them and ask God to bless them. It is a marvelous way to start and end each day.

The five parts of the Blessing as taught by Gary Smalley and John Trent in their books, The Blessing and The Gift of the Blessing, are:

Five parts of the Blessing:
{
Meaningful Touch
Spoken Message
Attach High Value
A Special Future
Active Commitment

1. Meaningful touch is similar to the Biblical expression of "laying on of hands." This is placing hands upon the recipient's head or shoulders. This could also be holding hands or sharing a hug with the person you are blessing. Meaningful touch blesses the person physically, emotionally and spiritually. There have been numerous research projects proving that a physical improvement actually takes place when a person is touched.

2. Spoken words have the power to build up or tear down ... bring life or death. It is important to speak words of blessings allowing the recipient to use the sense of sound as well as the sense of touch. It is unfortunate when a husband will bless his wife with a "silent prayer." His wife loses out on the benefit of hearing the affirming spoken word that creates a close bond with her husband.

3. The third part of the blessing is placing high value on the person. A word picture to describe the value of the person can be used. Such phrases as "strength of a lion" or "the gentleness of a dove" can be expressed.

4. Affirming something in the person's future could be as follows: "May your future be full of God's blessings of peace and joy." It is a blessing for a fulfilling life in the years to come. It can also be asking God to bless your family's health for the future.

5. The main part of a blessing is to commit the person to God's care. By pronouncing a blessing, you are also pledging a commitment to do everything possible to help the person you are blessing. As a husband blesses his wife, he can also pledge his lifetime commitment to her.

A Blessing soothes the physical, mental, emotional and spiritual person. It leads to seeking Salvation – both in the short term and for eternity.

An angry couple came to us for ministry one day. The wife was so angry toward her husband that she had stopped speaking to him. When they returned, after practicing the blessing assignment for two weeks, she was laughing. She declared, "It's very difficult to stay angry with someone who is asking God to bless you every day!"

Numbers 6: 24-26

The Lord bless you and keep you.
The Lord make his face to shine upon you, and be gracious to you;
The Lord lift up his countenance upon you, and give you peace.

Proverbs 31: 10-31 (Husbands, read this to your wife!)

A wife of noble character who can find?
She is worth far more than rubies.
Her husband has full confidence in her and lacks nothing of value.
She brings him good, not harm, all the days of her life.
She selects wool and flax, and works with eager hands.
She is like the merchant ships, bringing her food from afar.
She gets up while it is still dark; she provides food for her family and portions for her servant girls.
She considers a field and buys it; out of her earnings she plants a vineyard.
She sets about her work vigorously; her arms are strong for her tasks.
She sees that her trading is profitable, and her lamp does not go out at night.
In her hand, she holds the distaff and grasps the spindle with her fingers.
She opens her arms to the poor, and extends her hands to the needy.
When it snows, she has no fear for her household; for all of them are clothed in scarlet.
She makes coverings for her beds; she is clothed in fine linen and purple.
Her husband is respected at the city gate, where he takes his seat among the elders of the land.
She makes linen garments and sells them, and supplies the merchants with sashes..
She is clothed with strength and dignity; she can laugh at the days to come.
She speaks with wisdom, and faithful instruction is on her tongue.
She watches over the affairs of her household and does not eat the bread of idleness.
Her children arise and call her blessed; her husband also, and he praises her:
"Many women do noble things, but you surpass them all."
Charm is deceptive, and beauty is fleeting; but a woman who fears the Lord is to be praised.
Give her the reward she has earned, and let her works bring her praise at the city gate.

Bless your children:

"Lord, help her do her best in school today and treat others as she would have them treat her. Let Your light shine through her."

"Lord, give him the strength he needs to be a good team-mate and a worthy opponent. Help him to do Your will today."

Body
Labor
Emotional
Social
Spiritual
} = **BLESS**

Body: Thank God for blessings of good health. If there is a specific need, pray for His blessing of healing

Labor: Thank God for blessing you in the workplace and for your labor to bear fruit. If unemployed, it is an opportune time to ask for blessings of employment.

Emotional: Ask God for help in healing of any damaged emotions from your past. Also ask for blessings to keep your emotions in tune with God.

Social: Ask God to bless you with friends of His choosing. Also ask for blessings on your friends and neighbors.

Spiritual: Ask God for continued spiritual growth, which will deepen your walk with Him as well as with your spouse.

COMMITMENT
Ponder Page ...

1. Have you committed to a relationship of prayer with one another on a daily basis? (If not, start today!)

2. What prayer would you offer to God on behalf of your spouse this very day?

3. What will your marriage be like when you both commit to living in relationship with one another under God's grace? What will it be like if you do not?

Compassion

Compassionate couples love one another unconditionally.

They never condemn one another.

Rather, they continually bless one another

through prayer and forgiveness.

The healing power of prayer replaces hurt with compassion.

Compassion fills your heart and overflows.

Take the compassion of Christ with you.

Others will follow in your footsteps.

Pray Together, Compassionately, with love,

A minimum of Once A Day

Chapter Three

Compassion
The Marathon

The night sky was full of glittering stars, but Jack didn't notice them as he got in his car for the three-hour drive from Tallahassee to Jacksonville, Florida. A successful business executive and weekend marathon runner, Jack was at the lowest point of his life as he pulled his car onto the highway and headed for home. Home? What was that?

Without his wife and children, home didn't exist any more. "Well, what did I expect?" he thought sadly to himself. Gwen, his wife of 14 years, had discovered his extra-marital affair and kicked him out the week before. Jack was losing his family.

As he idly flipped through stations on the car radio, a deep, warm voice on an unfamiliar Christian station caught his attention. "Footprints in the Sand," announced the voice, reciting the famous words written by Mary Stevenson back in 1936:

One night I dreamed I was walking
Along the beach with the Lord.

Many scenes from my life flashed across the sky.
In each scene I noticed footprints in the sand.

Sometimes there were two sets of footprints.
Other times there was one set of footprints.

This bothered me because I noticed that
During the low periods of my life when I was
Suffering from anguish, sorrow, or defeat,
I could see only one set of footprints.

So I said to the Lord, "You promised me, Lord,
that if I followed You,
You would walk with me always.

But I noticed that during the most trying periods
Of my life there have only been one set of prints in the sand.

Why, when I have needed You most,
Have You not been there for me?"

The Lord replied,
"The times when you have seen only one set of footprints
Are when I carried you."

Jack pulled over to the side of the road, tears streaming down his face. "Oh, Lord," he prayed, his hands clutching the wheel and his heart beating out of control. "I need you to carry me now."

That night, Jack began running the biggest marathon of his life. Restoration of his broken marriage was at the finish line.

(Gwen): "When Jack and I got married, we had 'happily ever after' hopes and dreams. As the years went by, our two children were born, we did well financially, and a couple of years ago, we bought a new home. Jack is a devoted father and loves his children so much, but somewhere along the way, our relationship as husband and wife cooled down. I relied on Jack as my strength when both of our dads died during the past three years. We were full of compassion for one another when the chips were down, but it wasn't long before the coolness came back. When we began attending a new church as a family, I hoped we'd get closer, but we just continued to drift apart. On the surface, we looked like the All American family. The reality was that something was terribly wrong."

"I'm an independent, self-made man," explains Jack. "I worked my way through college and achieved financial success by the time I was 30." Running marathons, raising kids, and rising to the top in his profession were accomplishments that made Jack proud.

"Gwen didn't give me the attention I felt I deserved, so I found it elsewhere. When I look back now, I realize I was full of arrogance and false pride. No matter how I acted, she was there, loving me all along."

"Jack travels in his job. The more distant our relationship became, the more insecure I became," remembers Gwen. "I wasn't happy with my appearance, but I kept gaining weight, running up the charge cards, and pushing aside my gut instincts. One night we had a huge argument. I told him I suspected he was having an affair. He denied it, but admitted that he felt we were in a rut. The next day, he sent two-dozen roses to my office. That was when I knew in my heart that he was lying. Two dozen was too many. I've since learned to trust my instincts."

One lie led to another until, finally, Gwen insisted they seek Don and Anne's counsel at church. Although Jack willingly participated in the counseling sessions, he admits now that he was merely going through the motions in order to keep from losing his family.

Counseling revealed many factors that contributed to Jack's infidelity and Gwen's poor money management. Both of their fathers had been unfaithful in their marriages. "It was an old story of the sins of the fathers being revisited on their children," says Gwen. "It just didn't seem to be such a big deal to Jack. In the meantime, I was burying my resentment by piling up the bills and eating, instead of taking it to the Lord in prayer."

While making all sorts of surface gestures, like planning special parlor picnics with Gwen, sending flowers and writing love notes, Jack was still unwilling to let his extra-marital relationship end. "When I found out he was still calling her, even after we began counseling, that was it," said Gwen. "I kicked him out of the house and I told friends at church that it would take a miracle to save our marriage."

The miracle happened the night Jack got a radio message from God. "The words of 'Footprints in the Sand,' changed me," he says. "I felt like I'd been hit in the face with a brick. For the first time in my life, I realized I wasn't in control – had never been in control. God had been there all along, but I had never acknowledged Him. I'd been running the marathon called life and the only way I would make the finish line was with God by my side."

"It's strange," muses Gwen. "Don predicted that God would hit Jack with a spiritual two by four, and He did. When I finally agreed to talk with Jack again, he cried like a baby and confessed everything and promised to put Jesus in the center of our relationship. There was an aura of peace about him that I'd never seen before. I could see God's strength in his determination to make things work. I was filled with compassion and forgiveness for him. It was the miracle I'd prayed for."

"After a couple of visits with Don and Anne, I realized my self-worth was pretty rotten. With the betrayal, I felt rotten inside. They talked about God's compassionate forgiveness, but I continued to refer to myself as 'worthless.' Don advised that he would like to bring a tape player to our next meeting and allow God to minister to me with song."

During their time together the following week, Gwen listened to a recording called, "I Will Change Your Name".

"I will change your name,
You shall no longer be called wounded, outcast, lonely or afraid.
I will change your name,
Your new name shall be confidence, joyfulness, overcoming one,
Faithfulness, friend of God, One who seeks my face."

by D. J. Butler; Mercy Publishing, 1987
All Rights Reserved. Used with Permission.

*After allowing the enchanting words to penetrate her heart, Gwen joined Don and Anne in prayer, asking God to instill a new name for her in her heart and spirit. "The beautiful experience was that I heard so clearly God giving me a brand new name: **"HOPE."** I left that afternoon not only with a new name, but with new hope in my heart!"*

Together, one footstep at a time, Jack and Gwen are healing. "The hardest thing is learning to forgive myself," says Jack. "I carry the burden of guilt with me every day. I nearly destroyed my family. My mind gets going and then I force myself to stop and think about 'Footprints in the Sand.' It's bizarre that I found that radio station that night. I would not typically have been listening to a Christian station."

Jack and Gwen were recently baptized by full immersion at their church. It was beautifully described by Jack. "As a novice Christian, I never realized that by baptism you're buried dead to self under the water and then resurrected as a child of God," marvels Jack. "When I was baptized, I felt reborn. My soul and spirit were cleansed."

Putting Christ in the center of their marriage, blessing one another every day and praying together, Jack and Gwen have discovered the compassionate forgiveness God has for them. They are back on track. "As a marathon runner, I know we're still at the beginning stages of the race. It's a long marathon and it's like we're at mile 3 of a 26.2 mile run. Having that affair was not worth it. I never anticipated how overwhelming the guilt and anxiety would be – it was like I was running the marathon in army boots through mud. Now, with Gwen and the Good Lord carrying me, it's a team effort. The three of us will make it to the finish line."

Colossians 3: 12-14:

Therefore, as God's chosen people, holy and dearly loved, clothe yourself with compassion, kindness, humility, gentleness and patience. Bear with one another and forgive whatever grievances you may have against one another. Forgive as the Lord forgave you. And over all these virtues put on love, which binds them all together in perfect unity.

Colossians 3: 12-14 is the guide for all people in relationships. It will heal the wounds caused in a marriage relationship. We also suggest you read again the message of Dietrich Bonhoeffer found in the homily. GOD'S COMMAND IS TO CLOTHE YOURSELF WITH COMPASSION.

Recently, we found an acrostic of the word "h-e-a-r-t" that was published by The Atlanta Consulting Group, copyright 1991. The acrostic is:

H ear and understand me.
E ven if you disagree, please don't make me wrong.
A cknowledge the greatness within me.
R emember to look for my loving intentions.
T ell me the truth with compassion.

Note that when you get to the HEART of the matter, all Seven C's intermingle. When you "Hear and understand me," you are using compassionate communication. "Even if you disagree with me, please don't make me wrong," can be a costly concession on your part, but will lead to clear communication and conflict resolution. "Acknowledge the greatness in me," is a celebration of the commitment and covenant you share together and with God. To "Look for my loving intentions," requires compassion as well as a willingness to resolve conflicting emotions. "Telling me the truth with compassion," speaks volumes in the art of communication. Each of the Heart-streams flow into the larger C's and illustrate the necessity of sailing fully equipped.

The American Heritage Dictionary has an interesting definition of "compassion": "The deep feeling of sharing the suffering of another." We can also think of compassion as a deep love coming from commitment made by one person to another. Intimacy will reign out of this compassion. What a powerful insight we have for compassion when we look at the true meaning of this word as expressed by the dictionary! This is the compassion a husband and wife are to have toward one another and the compassion God has for each of His children as expressed through Jesus Christ! You are a child of The King, created by Him and in His image. So be it. You can deny it; you can run and hide as Adam and Eve did. Nevertheless, this is God's Truth.

Unconditional Love

God loves each one of us unconditionally — just as we are — certainly not as we think we should be nor as others think we should be. Our God loves each of us so much that He sent His only son to Earth to die for us. Through this act of compassion, He has set us free in order to reconcile us back to Himself ... Our Abba, Father ... our Daddy God. This is the identical sacrificial compassion that husbands are to have towards their wives. That is an awesome thought for the men! Ephesians 5:25 requires husbands to love your wives as Christ loves the church. What an incredible commitment! However, when the requirement is met, it works amazingly well. A relationship of unconditional love is formed that cannot be broken. Biblically speaking, a husband's love for his wife is to be Calvary Love, the sacrificial love of Jesus Christ on the cross at Calvary, a hill outside of Jerusalem where He was crucified. That is the covenant made on the wedding day, and an everlasting commitment flowing out of a true marriage relationship.

Five Stages of Marriage

    In Michele Weiner Davis' classic book, *The Divorce Remedy*, she lists the five stages of a marriage. The first stage she refers to as "Passion prevails" or that stage we sometimes call the honeymoon. Everything is lovey-dovey and you are head-over-heels in love.

    Stage two comes on the scene. Michele refers to this as the "What was I thinking?" stage. "Who is this person waking up next to me with such bad breath? Why won't he pick up his own clothes off the floor? What a slob I married. Why does she spend so much money?"

    Then comes stage three which is "Everything would be great if you would change." Isn't it amazing how we are attracted to the perfect spouse and then spend the rest of our lives attempting to change them into the image we want them to be? We waste so much time and energy in this stage trying to get our spouse to see everything our way. Of course, we think our way is the only way! Right?

    Then along comes stage four which is "That's just the way my partner is." This is the realization that I'm not going to change that "other" person, anyway. We also, hopefully, begin to realize that we are becoming more apt to forgive our spouse and ready to move on to the fifth stage of "Together at last."

    When we make it to stage five, we have come from "passion to compassion." We have made it to "The deep feeling of sharing the suffering and joy of another."

    Compassion should not be one-sided. Jesus' teaching was very clear when he said in John 8:32, "Then you will know the truth, and the truth will set you free." However, merely knowing the truth will not lead to freedom. Freedom comes when we become doers of the truth. In the same manner, merely knowing how husbands are to treat wives is not enough. Husbands are not just to "know" Ephesians 5:25. They are to "do" Ephesians 5:25.

    Likewise, compassion cannot be for the self-gratification of one spouse. Remember the definition we previously discussed. Compassion is "the deep feeling of sharing the suffering of another," and involves giving up of self for the sake of your spouse. This will be discussed further when we embark on the sea of cost.

Our Sexuality

Our sexuality is a gift from God. Our sexual guidelines are a gift from God. He expects us to adhere to these guidelines. God created sex for our pleasure in marriage and for a lifetime of enjoyment for a husband and wife. It is to be a Godly time of 100% giving and 100% receiving. Total enjoyment of making love for a husband and wife is the same as total commitment in marriage: to move from selfishness to selflessness.

Good communication in sex is important as well. Our spouse needs to be able to express needs as well as dislikes. It is also important to meet one another's needs as long as there is nothing offensive to either person. This may feel embarrassing, but open communication and response needs to take place. It is equally important to communicate creative romance with one another. As long as both husband and wife are in agreement, it is permissible to be creative in expressing your love through sex.

Remember that men and women are so different sexually. Generally speaking, women see sex as relational, and men see it as an event. Women are relationally stimulated while men are visually stimulated; women need time to "warm up" with soft affection. Men are stimulated instantly. Women are put in touch with sex through their emotions while men get in touch with their emotions through sex.

Be patient as you learn and grow with God and one another. Remember, if there seem to be problems, communicate with compassion! Perhaps your spouse experienced sexual abuse as a child. How did each of you learn about sex? Some girls learn from their mothers that sex is dirty. Others learn it as a duty to be performed. If there are problems in your marriage, seek Godly wisdom and counsel. Help is just a prayer away.

Infidelity

Most marriages will survive infidelity. Some will come out of the healing process even stronger than before the affair. However, it will take time, patience and hard work on all parts of the relationship.

If you are the wounded spouse, you will need to express the pain and feelings you are experiencing. You may need to ask questions about the affair. If so, your spouse needs to answer these questions. Even though the answers may not be what you want to hear, they cannot be buried. The "betrayer" will need to be honest with "I" statements explaining the reasons behind the affair.

For the perpetrator: In spite of what you may think at the time, God gave you your spouse as a gift from Him. Acknowledge this to Him in prayer, then ask God to forgive you for dishonoring His gift. Also remember that repentance is the first step toward forgiveness.

In order to eventually rebuild the trust that was destroyed, sincere remorse must be shown from the heart. This must not be merely a word exercise with "I'm sorry." Eventually, forgiveness must take place between you and your spouse as well as between the betrayer and God. It is important that you find a good Christian counselor or work through your pastor to pray and receive forgiveness. As growth continues to manifest, there will come a time to renew your wedding vows. However, this cannot be rushed. It can only take place when both of you are ready. We have witnessed the children of couples who were "lost in the sea of infidelity," joyfully participating as ring bearers in the renewing of wedding vows in the church.

If you are a Christian couple who has experienced infidelity, you need to go on the "attack mode" against Satan. This is done through the power of prayer and forgiveness. Satan wants to destroy your Christian marriage. An affair is one of the tools he uses to accomplish his task. Be prepared! Even when you are on the road to reconciliation, you may be bombarded with lies and doubt by the enemy. Gird yourselves for battle! Fight back with God's truth. Put on the full armor of God. In our experience, nearly 100% reconciliation occurs when couples are willing to work through the intense pain of adultery with God's strength, compassion and prayer.

Come-Passionate Prayer

Compassion and prayer are synonymous. Come-passionate prayer. This is more than grace at mealtime. Also, it is praying aloud! Some people are so uncomfortable with that, yet it is another habit that can be learned. Come out of your comfort zone – pray enthusiastically and visibly. Ask one another for any prayer needs for that day. Listen and pray with compassion. If you have children, pray with them and for your entire family.

Your children need your prayers even when they are forming in their mother's womb. Laying hands on the mother's stomach, pray for their safe passage into this world. Keep saying, " Whether you are a boy or a girl, we already love you and welcome you into this family." What a glorious way to begin introducing a child to God. As spiritual head of the family, men need to take this active role of prayer.

What Prayer Is: Prayer is conversation between two beings in love – you and God! The compassion of prayer is especially blessed when it is between three beings in love – you, your spouse, and God.

How To Do It: Talk to God honestly, respectfully, thankfully and from your heart, trusting Him completely.

We pray together each morning, compassionately and with deep love in our hearts for Jesus and for one another. We know Jesus is there, waiting for us, loving us unconditionally. Imagine that He is sitting in a chair by your front door. Would you walk by Him without saying Good Morning?

When we pray, we let Him know how much we love Him, how much we need Him and desire Him. Yet, the hardest part of prayer is LISTENING! How wonderful it would be if every couple spent time together listening for God's guidance. Most important, if you listen for God's compassionate response, you will know of His infinite love for you.

Prayer: ACTS – A = adoration
                          C = confession
                          T = thanksgiving
                          S = supplication

57

This is merely a tool to guide you through prayer. We are not suggesting you learn "techniques" to pray. For many of us, simply beginning to converse with our Heavenly Father is a good way to get started..

Adoration is expressing your overwhelming love for God. It may be as simple as saying, "Father God, I adore you with all my heart" or "I love you with all the love that is within me."

Confession is acknowledging that you, like all the rest of us, have "missed the mark." It is a time to confess your shortcomings. It is admitting that like all human beings, we are part of the fallen nature of man. You may desire to ask your Daddy God to forgive you of all your sins, known to you and unknown. This is always a way of being spiritually cleansed. We highly recommend that you always make this a part of your daily prayer.

Thanksgiving is self-explanatory. This is a time to thank your Lord for all that He has done for you, past, present and future. It is a time to recall all the blessings God has bestowed upon you. "Thank you God for _____."
(Fill in the blank)

Supplication is the act of humbly asking God for your needs in life. It is important to separate wants and needs at this point. It is fine to ask God to supply your needs. If your need is financial, for example, ask Him to bless you in this area if it is His will.

Now that we have sailed through the C's of *covenant, commitment and compassion*, we move into deeper bodies of living waters where we look at the crucial elements present in any solid marriage, those of *communication* and *conflict*.

Max Lucado's Wedding Prayer
(from *On the Anvil*):

THE WEDDING PRAYER

Create in us a love, O' Lord.
An eternal love … Your love.
A love that forgets any failure,
Spans any distance,
Withstands any tempest.

Create in us a love, O' Lord.
A new love,
A fresh love,
A love with the tenderness of a lamb,
The grandeur of a mountain,
The strength of a lion.

And make us one … intimately one.
As You made a hundred colors into a sunset,
A thousand cedars into one forest,
And countless stars into one galaxy …
Make our two hearts as one, Father, forever …
That You may be praised, Father, forever.

COMPASSION
Ponder Page ...

1. We are to clothe ourselves with compassion. When was the last time your spouse needed your compassion? Were you properly clothed?

2. Review the five stages of marriage found in this chapter. What stage are you in? What will it take on the part of each of you to get to Stage 5?

3. Are there unreasonable expectations you have placed on one another that need to be replaced with compassion, understanding and unconditional love? If so, what are they, and what can you offer to help with that process in order to bring understanding and peace?

Communication

We are in the midst of mass communication daily.

The Worldwide Web.

Radio, television, newspapers, books, music, art, dance

... all are means of communication.

Yet, sometimes we neglect

the most important forms of communication:

Communication with God.

Communication with our loved ones.

Communication with ourselves.

Remember, only God can teach us

the true art of communication.

Communication

Chapter Four

Communication

Valentine from Jesus

Bone-weary and six months pregnant, Janet lifted her 13-month-old son, Adam, out of the car seat, grabbed her purse and a small bag of groceries, pulled the mail from the mailbox, and struggled to unlock the door to her empty house. Janet had taken a sleepy Adam to daycare at 6:30 a.m. that chilly February morning and then worked a stressful 8-hour shift as a surgical technician assisting in a liver transplant. "Where is Richard when I need him?" she wailed silently as she tried to make Adam's bath a happy, quality time. "Poor baby," she thought. "His mom is too exhausted to play and his dad is almost a forgotten memory." Gently she put Adam in his crib and dragged herself to the living room, where she collapsed in a chair.

"I was at a real low point," she remembers. "Richard and I had been through so much turmoil in the past two years and then, just when it seemed that God had put our marriage on solid ground again, his Dad died."

As young newlyweds in Florida, Janet and Richard had enjoyed carefree days of golfing, roller-blading and volleyball at the beach. They had worked long hours saving up for their first home – she at the hospital and Richard as a restaurant manager. Eventually, they bought their house, found a good church, saw one another on and off between shifts, and, generally, lived what they considered "the good life." Their first conflict came when Richard's younger brother moved in. Both from large families in Ohio, they were devoted to their siblings. Richard's brother had come to Florida seeking help with a drug problem, but had, instead, gotten into the drug scene locally and was more addicted than ever. Having him in their home put a big strain on their relationship and, finally, they asked him to leave.

Their real troubles began when Janet was diagnosed with endometriosis. Although they had always planned to have children someday, they had decided to wait until they were better *established financially. Doctors advised them, in view of Janet's condition, not to wait. When Janet told Richard she was pregnant, he said he was thrilled, but as time went by, he began acting differently and spending longer hours at work. At first, it was difficult for Janet to believe the change in him. He went from being a loving husband to acting like he wanted nothing to do with her. Always quiet and "close-mouthed", Richard put up a wall of silence between them. When he transferred to a new restaurant across town, he began coming home very late at night, after he was sure Janet was asleep. They rarely saw one another any more. When Janet begged him to tell her what was wrong, Richard refused to answer, remaining cool and distant.*

One night, Janet waited up for him. He walked right past her and went into the bathroom to take a shower. Janet followed him. She talked through the shower curtain, begging him to tell her why he was acting the way he was; to tell her what she had done to make him change; to tell her what was wrong; how she could make things better .... her words floated in the air as the steamy shower continued and no answer came from behind the curtain of silence. Finally, Richard yanked the curtain aside and said, simply, "I just don't want to be married to you anymore."

Halfway through her pregnancy, Janet sat in a daze as he dried himself off and walked away. Her attempt at solid communication had not only failed – it seemed as though it had been the catalyst to slam their marriage on the jagged rocks of despair.

The next day, she began making phone calls. If she couldn't communicate with Richard, she was bound and determined to communicate with people about Richard. She called friends at church. She called Richard's friends and employees. She learned from one of Richard's employees that there was a new girl at work who had been pursuing him – bringing him dinner on her days off and openly flirting with him. She'd even been seen rubbing his back. Janet wasn't going to give up without a fight. She drove to the restaurant and walked straight back to Richard's office. When she opened the door, she found Richard and the "new girl" in his office talking intimately. She pointed her finger at the girl angrily and told her to get out. The girl left, but Richard sat silently, offering no explanation. He was as cold as ice.

Janet went home determined to save her family. She asked friends at church to pray for Richard. She told them that she and Richard were both from broken homes and that she knew, in her heart, Richard was a good man who did not want his children raised in a single-parent home. She prayed and cried and prayed and cried. For a while, she moved out of the house and lived with friends from church, leaving Richard to take care of the dog and the house and giving him the space he said he needed. After several weeks alone and many phone calls from church friends, Richard begged Janet to come home.

Together, they began seeing Don and Anne for marriage ministry, attending bible study, and little by little, renewing their relationship. Richard still remained silent most of the time, but he told Janet that he wanted to make their marriage work. Ministry revealed that the prospect of parenthood had terrified him. He told Don and Anne that he had been full of doubt about his faith in God and jealous of Janet's close relationship with church friends and her reliance on prayer. He did, however, admit that his faith in God was getting stronger after seeing Janet's willingness to stay and fight for their marriage instead of leaving him flat, as he felt he deserved.

Janet felt that God had intervened just in time that night she waited up and talked on the other side of the silent shower curtain. Her attempt at communication had, indeed, succeeded. It had begun the process of healing. Whatever Richard had done or contemplated doing, he was back on the right path and now working toward being the husband and father he was meant to be. Her heart was full of forgiveness and hope.

When Adam was born, Richard and Janet brought him into the world together. Long, sleepless nights with a newborn, diaper changes and new parental responsibilities kept them busy at home. Richard worked long hours and, soon, Janet was back at work. Their hectic schedules made continued quality communication nearly impossible. They were together, though, and Janet prayed it would stay that way.

When Richard's father died, he took it very hard. Verbal, for once, he railed against God that his dad had died an untimely death so far away. All of his childhood memories flooded back (both negative and positive) and he left for his father's funeral in a state of deep depression.

Now, weeks after the funeral, Richard was still back home in Ohio and Janet sat alone in the quiet house, a sleeping baby in the crib and another moving fitfully inside her. "It was a dark night for me," said Janet. "I was worried about Richard's faith in God. I was worried about whether our marriage could survive another upheaval and another pregnancy."

As she sat listlessly sorting through the mail, she opened the weekly church newsletter.

Her eyes widened as she gazed at the beautiful illustration of Jesus there, and read John 3:16, "For God so loved the world that He gave His only Son, that whoever believes in Him should not perish but have eternal life." Suddenly realizing that it was Valentine's Day and she'd been too preoccupied by work and worry to even notice, Janet began to smile.

"It was a Valentine from Jesus! Just when I needed it the most." Energized by God's incredible timing, Janet was not surprised when the phone rang. It was Richard.

"We had our first good conversation in months that night," she recalls. "We talked for hours. I told him how much I loved him. He told me how much he loved me. I told him about the Valentine and we marveled at how much God loves us. Somehow, I knew then that everything was going to be alright."

Today, Janet and Richard are the parents of two fine sons. "God is the glue that held us together. The most important thing is to have faith, keep praying, and stay in close communication with the family of God. I don't think Richard and I would be together today if I hadn't asked the people of the church to pray for him. When you think you can't pray any longer – just keep praying, and when trouble hits hard – like the death of Richard's dad – and things seem so dark, God will communicate with you. He will send a sign to light the way. The Valentine from Jesus was just such a sign. Our faith has become so strong as a result of the tests our marriage has survived. Now God uses us for testimony to other troubled couples. It's easy to walk away when trouble strikes – the true test is in trusting in the marriage covenant we made before God. Richard has learned to communicate with me, and even in the quiet times, I know he is communicating with God in prayer."

Internet Overflow

Laura was addicted to internet dating. "I discovered that you could type in whatever qualities you were looking for in a man – height, weight, hair color, eye color, occupation, religious status - and boom! – he would appear before your eyes. I must have dated 30 or 40 men that I met over the internet, and I had e-mail lists of my favorites in reserve for more dates, but it always turned out the same. The ones I liked didn't like me. The ones that liked me, I didn't like. There was so much heartache in it. Every date seemed to break me down more and it seemed like I'd never find love." Laura had been chasing that elusive thing called love all her life. Raised in a home where there was little physical contact and even less verbal reassurance of love, Laura grew up feeling unlovable.

"My mother worked hard, put food on the table and a roof over our heads. That was her way of showing love. The only times I can ever remember her showing any kind of emotions were when I was in some kind of deep, traumatic situation. Otherwise, she was cold as ice." As teenagers, Laura and her sisters had no rules. They could do anything they liked as long as they didn't bother their mother. "We didn't even have the love of discipline," she recalls. "There was absolutely no love language spoken in our house." When Laura was 14, she endured sexual abuse by her stepfather, but by then she was so damaged emotionally that the physical abuse hardly touched her. Emotionally, she had built a wall that was nearly impenetrable. She regularly escaped to a fantasy land where she felt that all of her dreams were destined to come true.

"I always knew in my heart that if I ever married, it would be forever, and it would be to the man of my dreams. But since I didn't really know what love was, the man of my dreams was pure fantasy. As soon as I detected any imperfection in a boy, the relationship was instantly over. I felt you should be swept off your feet and live happily ever after – just like in the movies."

In Laura's mind, real love was out there somewhere, and she was determined to find it. "My daughter, Tiffany, was the result of a short-term relationship with a man I met in a bar when I was 21. He wasn't the Prince Charming I was seeking, though, so it never entered my mind to marry him, even though he took responsibility for paying child support and became a permanent part of my daughter's life."

Raising a daughter on her own, and still searching for Mr. Right, Laura dated man after man that she met on the internet. "That's how I met William. He was just another man I'd put on my buddy list as a possibility. After we e-mailed a few times, we went to phone conversations. Talking with him was easy, so I decided to meet him."

William and Laura met at a local bar for a drink. The next day, he called and asked for a date.

William was just as romantic as the movie heroes Laura had always dreamed about. He took her to expensive restaurants. He took her to Disney World. For her 29th birthday, he arranged for a weekend of horseback riding and got a room at a fancy bed and breakfast. "He just did everything he could to sweep me off my feet. He even showered my daughter with love and affection. I was hooked. Here was the true love I'd waited for all my life." Now that Laura had everything she had ever dreamed of, she was determined not to lose it. She became extremely possessive and jealous of every minute that William spent away from her. She began to call him incessantly, smothering him to the point that, within three months, he broke up with her.

"That was when I started going to church. I fell at the altar, just sobbing, and begged God to make me worthy of William's love. I poured myself into church activities and joined the drama ministry. It was the beginning of my relationship with God."

One day, Laura sent William a single rose and a note asking for another chance. It worked. William not only came back into her life, but he joined the church and the drama ministry. "When I look back at it now, I realize that I still had not learned how to love," recalls Laura. "As soon as William was back in my life, I began playing silly games and pushing him away. I was even jealous of his new involvement in my church. True love was staring me in the face, and I didn't know how to handle it."

After breaking up and going back together several times, Laura and William moved into a house together and began to make plans to get married. "By then, we had become friends," remembers Laura. "I had never been friends with a man who showed me unconditional love, but I found it with William." But Laura's outward semblance of contentment was again plagued by doubt. What if William wasn't the one? Did she really love him enough to marry him? She loved him, but was she IN love with him? She struggled continually with conflict in her heart. "I thought love was a feeling, not a choice. I began doubting my feelings."

Then Laura became pregnant. With pregnancy came hormonal changes that wreaked havoc in their lives. "You can call it what you will, but I know it was Satan. He was working overtime, bringing up my past and echoing in my head, 'You don't love him, you don't really love him. You can't marry him.' I got nasty. I did everything in my power to push William away." Laura began to be repulsed by William's touch. "He could just put his hand on my leg and it would send chills up my body. I was so cold and mean to him, and he just stayed by me and kept saying he loved me. One night in bed, I sat up and told him I couldn't marry him. I took off my ring and gave it back to him. He shot straight up in bed and cried, 'Oh my God, I just heard Satan laugh!'"

For months, in spite of the progression of her pregnancy, Laura felt empty inside. She listened to sermons and read the Bible and prayed to God for affirmation that she was doing the right thing. She went to Don and Anne for counseling. They urged her to listen to God's will regarding parenting and family. They expressed deep concern for her determination to raise her children as a single mother. William went, too. He told Don and Anne that he was crying out to God, begging Him to change Laura's heart.

At about seven months pregnant, Laura was driving in her car and found herself screaming at God. "I can't change! You can't make me love him now. If you want me to love him, you need to create a miracle, because I can't do it!" As soon as she shouted those words, Laura remembers an incredible peace coming over her. "There was a stillness. I could actually hear God asking, 'Are you finished? Now, can I go to work?'"

Laura called William and asked him to go with her again to meet Don and Anne. They prayed together and Laura's true healing began. "He put it on my heart that love was a choice – not a feeling – and from that point on, it was incredible. I made the choice to love William. At first, I had to fake it and pretend that I enjoyed him touching me. It got easier and easier as God showed me how to love."

Little by little, Laura learned that she had never truly loved anyone. "I had been raising Tiffany the same way my mother raised me. Oh, I always made sure and told her I loved her, because that's something I remembered my mother never doing, and I let her sleep in my bed when she was young, but whenever she reached out to me, I recoiled. I never gave her real time. Whenever she asked me to do something, I'd say 'In a minute' and push her away, just like my mother used to do. In fact, it wasn't just Tiffany – it was anybody. I wouldn't let anybody break down my walls."

Their daughter was six months old when William and Laura got married. Don and Anne performed the ceremony. "The walls are gone now," says Laura. "We have the marriage that God intended. It's not a fantasy. It's real. I wish I could bottle and sell the joy we have and share it with everyone."

By praying together and putting Christ in the center of their marriage, William and Laura have learned to communicate on an intimate level. "I've always had a problem with intimacy. It isn't about sex – that's an act – it's about spiritual intimacy. The more intimate we become spiritually, the more naked I become to William, and the more oneness we experience. Before I gave myself to God, there was a huge hole in my heart. Now it is filled to overflowing."

Proverbs 25:11
A word gently spoken is like apples of gold in settings of silver.

It was difficult to choose a scripture when it comes to "communication." There are approximately 64 proverbs pertaining to speaking or listening. We also point to references from the book of James about the tongue bringing life or death. However, there is something special and very descriptive in the possibility of our spoken words being like "apples of gold in settings of silver."

Karen Hughes, a former speechwriter for President Bush, beautifully expressed the importance of selecting affirming life-giving words. Her comment was, "Words are the currency of our relationships." Yes, our words are, indeed, to be apples of gold in settings of silver.

The words and actions that we use to communicate with our spouse are so vitally important that, when misused, they can create dangerous barrier reefs that, if not detected early enough, can capsize the vessel of marriage. This is particularly true when those words and actions relate to financial instability, sexual dysfunction or marital infidelity.

Many marriage therapists believe financial matters are the biggest cause of marriage breakups. This is true in some cases. However, if there are solid gold communication skills in place, the conflict of finances can be resolved. Go to the root of the problem – go for the gold and communicate honestly!

The same holds true for problems with sexuality. Good, solid communication is absolutely in order to express your needs and desires as well as to let your spouse know what may offend you when dealing with sexuality. Sex is a gift from God and can be as luscious as the sweetest apple, especially when the body language is communicated well.

As to infidelity, we can assure you that to affair-proof your relationship, it is essential to learn good communication skills. Allow one another to openly express feelings as well as thoughts. It is when one spouse appears not to be a good listener that Satan will place someone in the path of the one who needs to express their hurt or pain. When a good listener of the opposite sex comes along, an emotional affair may be birthed. This begins innocently, but has the potential to bring disaster into the marriage as it often can develop into a physical affair.

We have sailed through three of the Seven C's and our boat has not capsized! However, be assured that the seas will get rougher. It is now time to put our knowledge to work in order to acquire our "sea (C) legs."

As previously mentioned, it is our belief that issues are not the primary problems in marriage - rather, it is the lack of skills to deal with the issues. Without these basic skills, you are attempting to catch the breeze to move your boat along, and you do not even have your sails extended! Lack of sails makes it necessary to row – a labor that can exhaust you before communication ever begins. So, begin to lift your sails and catch the wind of the Holy Spirit as we sail into the sea of Communication. Just as our navigational compass seeks magnetic North, we need to constantly seek win-win outcomes through good communication.

"I" Statements

Be a good listener and be a good speaker. Use "I" statements.

As far as good skills are concerned, all dialogue is to express *your* needs and desires. This is accomplished with "I" statements rather than "you" statements. By using "I" expressions, you are making your desires known and taking ownership of your thoughts and feelings. If you choose to use "you" statements, it will probably come across as accusatory and your spouse may become defensive and withdraw. Allow your spouse to feel at ease expressing "I" statements, as well. It is important for both of you to feel safe with one another in order to confide your innermost thoughts and feelings without fear of rejection or ridicule. In other words, you need to be one another's "safe harbor".

Too often, a "you" statement can be considered "finger pointing," which leads to attack and counterattack. This method is also used in attempting to control the situation. You are focusing upon the other person rather than yourself.

On the other hand, with "I" statements, you are focusing upon yourself. This type of communication is non-threatening and will lead to an atmosphere of acceptance and understanding. It opens the conversation to inner feelings that need to be shared and used to build trust. Blame is a pirate that plunders our ship at sea. Blame blocks healing and reconciliation. "I" statements eliminate blame.

No Buts...

Keep your communication open with one another, unconditionally, and with no "buts, shoulds or what if's." In fact, work on breaking the habit of inappropriately using the word "*but.*" Too often we tell one another "I love you, *but* ... you are sloppy, you are lazy, you are overweight, you are extravagant, you are insensitive, you are abusive, you are ..." (fill in the blank...)

We even tell our children we love them, *but* their grades need to be better, and on and on. The word "*but*" negates what precedes it. The word "*but*" puts conditions upon the love. It takes time to break the "*but*" habit, just as it does with all habits. You and your spouse can work together to remind one another, lovingly, that part of your communication with one another is "No Buts Allowed."

Exchange

Our reliable dictionary definition of communication is "the exchange of thoughts, messages or information." We suspect that the word, "exchange" infers that there needs to be at least one other person involved. How often we as husbands and wives forget the need for two individuals to communicate! Many of us communicate with the following style: "*I know you believe you understand what you think I said, but I'm not sure you realize that what you heard is not what I meant.*" Just like a solid marriage, good communication skills take hard work!

Strong marital communication is the ability to express your desires and needs to your spouse in a non-threatening manner. This is not in the sense of beginning an argument. Arguments usually lead to someone becoming defensive and can further lead to unresolved conflict. One of humorist Will Rogers expressions was "*There's two theories to arguing with a woman. Neither one works.*" No need going there! Learn to approach communication with these non-threatening tools. Yes, it really can be done!

Verbal vs. Non-Verbal

The first step is to express yourself both verbally and non-verbally. Non-verbal communication is tone of voice and/or body language which is 85% of the total method of transmitting your message. Only 15% of your communication is represented by the actual spoken word.

If one spouse looks disgusted, rolls their eyes, looks up at the ceiling, down to the floor, has arms crossed and locked, slouches in a chair or watches TV during conversation, that person is loudly saying, "I'm not interested in you," or "What you have to say is not important" which translates to "You are not important." However, good eye contact or even bending slightly forward in your chair from a sitting position will show you have a keen interest and desire to hear what is being said.

(Anne): I was so impressed with Don's reaction when I needed to speak with him while he was engrossed in a St. Louis Cardinals baseball game. As a native of St. Louis, he has always been a fan of the Cardinals! This game was indeed important to him. Trying to be considerate, I asked if this was a good time in the game to ask him a question. I certainly did not want him to miss an important play. At that moment he actually turned off the TV. Wow! His action conveyed to me that I was more important to him than the ball game or the St. Louis Cardinals! I cannot begin to tell you how truly loved and important and validated I felt by Don because of his loving gesture.

Repetition/Affirmation

There are three parts to good communication. The method is as follows: Your spouse makes a statement to you. You repeat back to your spouse what you perceive was said, pausing for an affirmation from your spouse that the message was, indeed, correctly received. If affirmed, then the three-part process is complete. If your spouse fails to affirm that the message was correctly received, the communication process begins again. This may sound a bit offbeat, and yet it is the only sure way to achieve sound communication. It will feel awkward at first; however, in time it will become automatic, and create an atmosphere of understanding which will lead to better communication.

(Don): This reminds me of my days of instrument flying. Every clearance from the air controller had to be repeated back to them. This is the only way the controller knew if I had received it correctly. If it was incorrect, I had to go back to step one and begin again. This procedure kept me — and others — from getting into serious trouble since lives were at stake! It will also keep you out of trouble in your conversations with your spouse. Your marriage could be at stake!

We next need to understand the type of "filter" our spouse uses to receive messages. This is why it is imperative that you and your spouse understand one another's background and childhood.

Filters:

(Don): I grew up during the depression era and was part of a very loving and supportive family. Because of the lack of monetary security, I could have had an outlook of despair, yet picked up from my parents a "filter" of hope and optimism. I do, however, still have a hard time when it comes to spending money due to fear of money running out before our lives do. There is still a need to save for the rainy day.

(Anne): I grew up with unlimited finances and belonged to a mother who made me feel unwanted, unloved and in her way. My "filter" is one of guilt and shame because I was constantly criticized and felt I could do nothing right. I believed I was an intrusion. However, when spending summers with with my grandparents in Seattle when I was little, they loved me, as did the servants. The cook would even let me stand on a stool to help stir the food. She made me feel important, as did the rest of the servants. When living with my Great Aunt Anne in Wisconsin, for the first time, I felt truly accepted and valued, by both Aunt Anne and the servants. Her chauffer even helped fill the hole in my heart where Dad was absent. My beloved Aunt Anne loved me unconditionally, just like Jesus! What an incredible everlasting gift from my beloved Daddy God!

(Don): Anne and I had a situation between the two of us that may help to illustrate her low self-image. I had misplaced a teaching video in our home. I asked her to be on the lookout for it in case she saw it in her household endeavors. I was saying to her, "Anne, do not stop what you are doing. I'm only asking you to let me know if you stumble across it."

(Anne): What went into my negative filter was, "I must stop whatever I am doing to find this for Don. I don't think I am the one who misplaced it, and I hope I'm not in trouble!"

(Don): When I saw Anne drop what she was doing at that time, I knew her guilt filter had kicked into high gear. I said to Anne, "I really do not want you to stop what you are doing to look for this. It is NOT that important, and not worthy of guilt! Now repeat back to me what you heard me say."

(Anne): "I understand that you do NOT want me to specifically search for the video, and it is NOT my fault that it is missing."

(Don): "That is correct. Thanks." Then we hugged.

The rest of the story: God is always at work! As soon as Anne was released from her perceived thoughts that she had to find the video, God's quiet inner voice told Don to look in the lower drawer of their filing cabinet. That is where he found the "lost treasure!" Although the "rest of the story" doesn't always have such a positive outcome, the method of communication described above is always effective.

How did your parents communicate?

We all have different levels of communication skills. This is based primarily on how we heard our parents communicate with one another. Was this a positive or negative experience for you? Did you witness your parents shouting or accusing one another? Perhaps one of your parents used the silent treatment. What have you learned from your parents about ways to communicate? Anne was taught: "Children should be seen and not heard." Did you receive this message? What does that teach? No matter what we learned growing up, we can establish new habits and new thought patterns. We need to say "yes" to God and seek His help for positive change, which will instill self-confidence and raise self-esteem.

Ponder the following questions to get an understanding of how you handle communication: When there was conflict in your family, how did your mother and father speak to one another? How did they react to one another? What was your reaction? Was your family close-knit or was it a family that often "walked on eggshells?" Was your family highly organized or very disorganized and erratic? Are there any characteristics of your family that you mirror in your own style of communication? Which of these characteristics are positive and which are negative? What characteristics do you desire to bring into this relationship and which do you wish to leave behind? Are you willing to begin anew and learn new communication skills?

Daily Temperature Reading from PAIRS

Virginia Satir developed a fabulous communication tool for couples now called the "D.T.R." The following is an explanation of the D.T.R. First is the physical attitude of sitting and facing one another, knee to knee and eye to eye.

As you hold hands, the husband usually starts by telling his spouse one to two things he APPRECIATES about her. This should not be something general, such as "You are a great wife!" Be specific. "I appreciate that you took out the trash last night," or "I appreciate the awesome effort you put into that fabulous dinner last night." You get the idea?

Second step of the husband is to share any NEW INFORMATION to discuss. (If no thoughts of new information come to mind, just pass on this at that time.). New information is the way to keep connected with what is going on in your life. "I read an interesting article today about … Or "I'm considering making a doctor's appointment about my sinus problem." "I heard our next door neighbor may be moving." It can also concern something about you as a couple or your extended family.

The third step to the D.T.R. is to share any PUZZLEMENTS you have. "I'm puzzled that you seem unhappy today." Or, "I'm puzzled you were so quiet last night." "I'm puzzled I was passed over for a promotion at work." This is a time to express freely without debate what may be bothering you. If you do not have any puzzlements, simply pass.

Next, the husband is to share CONCERNS WITH REQUESTS FOR CHANGE. Too often we tell our spouse what we do not like. This is a time to share what you would like to see changed in your relationship. Remember, the other person may choose not to change – it's just a way to express what you would like to see happen. Be specific with this request. It is NOT a time for attack, blame or judgment, but only an expression of what would help you. Again, it is fine to pass on this as well.

Finally, share your WISHES, HOPES AND DREAMS with your wife. Sharing your dreams draws you closer together. A spouse who understands your hopes and dreams will draw you together in prayer as you work together. As you grow older, these may change. However, this, and APPRECIATIONS should never be a "pass." When you, the husband, are finished, then your wife will go through the same process. When you both have completed, it's time for a hug and a kiss!

Tools

While we have shared a few communication techniques with you, we also refer you to some suggested readings in the bibliography for some great books for your "tool box." An effective method for sound and balanced communication skills can be found in Howard Markham, Scott M. Stanley & Susan Blumberg's book, *Fighting For Your Marriage."* The authors have named this skill the "Speaker/Listener Communication Technique." *Marriage Savers* also teaches this method in their workshops and in PAIRS Seminars that are held throughout the United States. We highly recommend this communication technique to you.

Briefly, the "Speaker/Listener Communication Technique" is similar to the "mirroring" or "parroting" method, but goes much deeper. It is a skill that designates one of you as the listener and one as the speaker. The speaker will symbolically hold an object in their hand to indicate they are the speaker. The listener can only listen, and needs to mirror what the speaker is saying. Feelings and thoughts are to be expressed without any disagreement or interruption. The listener is to do only that – listen, and not be preparing a rebuttal. Remember, the listener has to mirror back what the speaker is saying and needs to concentrate. After several statements are made by the speaker, the symbol is handed off to the listener who now will become the speaker. The goal now is to repeat what you heard. When this is clear, it is then your turn to express your thoughts and feelings.

And speaking of symbols, there was one couple that chose to use a floor tile as the symbol they exchanged during Speaker/Listener Communication, signifying which of them had "the floor." Our friend and fellow conference speaker, the late Ruth Carter Stapleton (sister of President Jimmy Carter) said she used a salt-shaker for this purpose. Think of an item in your life that has some significance and use it for this unique communication tool.

This could become your new family tradition. If you have children, the Speaker/Listener Communication technique is a fun, effective tool for the entire family. Allow your children to choose the symbol for exchange.

Are Women from Venus? Are Men from Mars?

Keep in mind there is also a difference in the way males and females communicate. Often, women just desire to vent their feelings and are only looking for their husbands to be good listeners. However, men are determined to be the "fixers" and want to jump right in and take care of the situation. Guys will get to the heart of the problem — even if women are not seeking help! Men are more into thoughts than feelings.

For instance, a husband and wife invite another couple over for dinner. The male guest asks the question, "Where did you get this steak?" Invariably, the husband's reply will go something like this: "We got it at that new meat market down the street." The wife will probably respond by asking, "Why, what's wrong with it?"

For those of you who are dads, you know how your daughters have the instinct to "speak with their eyes." I do not know of a father who hasn't melted when his daughter approaches him wanting something and stares into her daddy's eyes! It has to be a girl thing — and it works! Our communication skills are definitely different. It's one of God's blessings, as long as we understand the difference.

Levels of Communication

Experts in the field of communication tell us there are five levels of communicating to another person.

PHRASES: "How are you?" "Have a great day."
FACTS: "The football team is winning this season." "It's so humid out today."
OPINIONS: "I could never do that again." "I don't think that will work."
FEELINGS: "I feel hurt by what just took place." "I am frightened by the news."
NEEDS: "I really need to share something with you." "I need a hug right now."

Unfortunately, most marriages do NOT get past level three. It is imperative to get past the "opinion" level and share feelings and needs with one another. It is impossible to meet someone's needs when their feelings are not expressed openly!

Another tip: Learn to communicate with your spouse on the same level they are using. We usually express ourselves in one of three ways:

1. We speak in a visual mode. Examples are expressing thoughts as "I see what you are saying," "I see your pain," "That looks good to me," "It's kind of hazy to me right now."

2. We speak in an auditory mode. Examples are: "It sounds good to me," "I hear your pain," "That's loud and clear to me," "I hear what you are saying."

3. We also speak in a feeling mode. Examples of this are: "I feel your pain," "I sense you are upset about this," "My heart feels your disappointment."

Listen up!

Listening is the most difficult part of communication. The following are some important listening guidelines:

1. Listen carefully with your goal being to understand what is being said.
2. Although we are to listen with a plan to respond, do not concentrate on your response until the other person has completed expressing their thoughts.
3. Look at your spouse eye to eye. Express your good intentions to understand. It helps to hold hands and sit knee-to-knee.
4. Do not interrupt or try to complete the other person's sentences.
5. Ask questions to show interest.
6. Listen for what is *not* being said.
7. Be aware of body language.
8. "Parrot" or "mirror back" what you believe was said.

Remember, God gave us two ears and only one tongue. We are to listen more than we talk! Listen with empathy. Do this by paying attention with your eyes and with body language. Finally, do not come to any premature conclusions while you are listening.

The 5 Languages of Love

Words of Affirmation
Quality Time
Acts of Service
Physical Touch
Receiving Gifts

One of the exercises you might find enlightening is to list your needs in order, using the 5 Languages of Love. What is most important to you? Is it physical touch? Receiving gifts? Spending quality time together? Getting help with the housework? Receiving words of endearment?

Gary Chapman's book, *The Five Love Languages, How to Express Heartfelt Commitment to Your Mate,* has helped many couples learn to communicate with their spouse on a different level, using Chapman's five languages of love. Do you know what your spouse's primary love language is? Too often, we attempt to communicate love from our own need rather than from that of our spouse. What you are transmitting may not be what your spouse is receiving. There is no mystery involved in learning your spouse's primary love language. Simply ask ... then apply!

Gifts

If your spouse's prime expression of love is gift giving, please keep in mind that gifts do not have to be expensive. During premarital counseling, when we ask couples about their primary love language, one or the other is often surprised to discover that their future spouse loves to receive gifts. This is often the result of growing up in a family where Dad brought home gifts to show love because he was away on business so much. This is one more example of the importance of learning about your spouse's family of origin.

Service
Service is the act of doing something special for your spouse. During the early stages of dating or courtship, we can't seem to do enough for that special person! We desire to serve. However, after a year or so of marriage, we may revert back to what we learned about expressing love when we were growing up. Remember, even if it is your primary love language, it may not be your spouse's primary need.

Time
To spend quality and quantity time together is the third language of love. This is manifested in spending time together just being … just enjoying God's creation together, feeling His peace and joy. Take turns planning ways to spend special time together. It is also fun to surprise one another with periodic dates for just the two of you. Perhaps this involves being together to watch a sunset or sunrise without words even being spoken.

(Anne): Since Don and I work together, he will sometimes go to another area of the church to call and ask for a date. Cute!

Touch
With touch as the primary language of love, one needs to be certain to know the difference between love and lust. There really is such a thing as "soft affection." This is touch that does not lead to sex. All of us need to honor our spouse as to what kind of touch is preferred.

Words
There is a fallacy we all learn as children. *"Sticks and stones may break my bones, but words will never hurt me."* The complete opposite is true. Words can be utterly, completely and devastatingly damaging. Conversely, kind words can flow life and love into a person. Personal words of love can penetrate to the depths of our being, which brings us back to the words that can either bring life or death to our relationship.

*Northfield Publishing, copyright © 1992, 1995 by Gary D. Chapman. Summarized with permission.

All five of the languages of love are necessary. We thrive on each of them, yet one will be predominant. Discovering your spouse's primary language of love does not eliminate use of the others. They are all part of your journey on the Seven C's!

Discover the language of love that is most important to you. Both of you list the five love languages in order of their priority in your life and what you believe are your spouse's priorities. Then compare your lists to determine the primary love languages for each of you that will enhance your relationship. Ask your spouse if you are correct in your perception of their needs. You may be surprised to discover that your needs are very different from those of your spouse, or that the needs of your spouse are very different than you thought.

An important facet of communication and one that can be employed to enhance your relationship and produce a win-win situation regardless of your differences is compromise. When you and your spouse speak different languages of love, compromise is the key to becoming bilingual. Since our first impulse is to stand our ground and demand to get our way, the challenge here is to prayerfully consider the needs and desires of our partner; to avoid the unhappy deadlock that results from lack of communication and compromise. Just as top corporate negotiators learn to compromise – each giving and taking until a mutual agreement is made, you and your spouse can learn to compromise through open, honest communication with one another and with your Lord.

Now that your sails have caught the breeze of communication, you can more confidently continue on your voyage into the sea (C) of solving conflict.

COMMUNICATION
Ponder Page ...

1. Help one another make a list of non-verbals you use when communicating. What are you willing to give up? To change?

2. Does your communication with one another reach the depths of your feelings... your thoughts... your needs? If not, how will you reach those depths? Will you share your wishes, hopes and dreams… **or simply wait for the daily temperature?**

3. Practice "parroting" or "mirroring" together until you are both clear as to what is actually being communicated. Pick a subject and do this now.

4. Before moving on, be sure to discuss and compare your primary and secondary love languages.

Conflict

Conflict is unavoidable.

Our Lord strengthens us through conflict.

When faced with conflict,

our response determines the outcome.

Resolve to deal with conflict prayerfully and positively.

Conflict

Chapter Five

Conflict
Hitting a Homerun for God

Greg had been a professional baseball player most of his married life. In fact, it was baseball that brought Ginny and Greg together. "We were both coaching at a baseball and softball summer camp when we met," recalls Ginny. "My family knew Greg, as he'd coached my little brother and sister at the camp for years. Greg was still in college when we met and I was finishing college. I'm three years older than he is, but that never seemed to make a difference. We were great together."

Ginny and Greg had the dream marriage. "Friends were always asking for our secret," remembers Greg. "We were best friends and lovers. We were awesome together. It didn't matter if we were with other people or if it was just the two of us, Ginny always cracked me up with her sense of humor. She's very emotional and intelligent – always asking questions and seeking answers. I love that in her. She challenged and excited me. We never ran out of things to say to one another. We would have been happy shipwrecked on a deserted island."

For the first four years of their marriage, Greg was out of town playing baseball four to six months annually, while Ginny, an elementary school teacher, kept the home fires burning. Both raised in the Methodist Church, Ginny and Greg found a church home in Jacksonville, and attended regularly when he was in town. Ginny taught at a Christian school. They were a young couple that seemed to have all their priorities where they belonged, but they were later to discover that their Christian faith had been only on the surface and certainly not in the center of their marriage.

"I loved Greg passionately," says Ginny. "Baseball was his life and it was important to me that he was following his dream. Even though there were nights when I'd cry myself to sleep because I missed him so much, our time together when he came home was truly awesome. As far as all the women out there who are attracted to professional athletes, I didn't worry.

Greg was known as the baseball player who didn't party. He was very popular, very friendly, and very married."

When Greg was injured, his baseball career came to an end. He landed a job as a personal trainer at a local fitness facility, and took on additional jobs to bring in extra income. "I'd always dreamed of the time when he would come home every night," said Ginny, "I thought that was when our real married life would begin. We'd have a house and children and live happily ever after, but it didn't work out that way." The reality was that Greg left the house at 6 a.m. and sometimes didn't get home until after 10 p.m.

Ginny would come home from teaching and find that she still carried the load of all of the household chores alone. Working long hours to make a good life for his family, Greg would fall into bed at night, exhausted. The open communication they had once enjoyed was replaced with silence, and then resentment. Neither Greg nor Ginny felt fulfilled.

When Greg filled that void with another woman, their marriage capsized in a dark, downward spiral that nearly drowned them in a sea of despair.

"It started out as friendship," Greg explains. "She was a pretty prominent lady in the community and I was proud to be her personal trainer. We got along so well that we started meeting to talk together after working out. She had some issues with her marriage and, since I'd retired from baseball and come home, Ginny had changed."

"I had changed," says Ginny, "and so had Greg. I was working in a Christian environment and beginning to understand where God belonged in our lives, while Greg was working in a totally secular place, where the values were very different. Everything in the workout facility centered around how fit you were. If you didn't eat right, your day was ruined. People were judged on their appearance. It was not a giving, loving place – it was all about physical fitness and self. While Greg was working out and listening to loud rap music blaring all around him, I was walking down the halls of the school as Christian music played softly, doing Bible lessons with my kids and pulling closer to God. We were in opposite worlds. I could feel Greg slipping away."

Ginny knew a lot of Greg's clients, including the woman with whom he was having an affair. When she began suspecting that there was more than a business relationship between them, she confronted Greg and he repeatedly denied it, becoming angry and verbally abusive for the first time in their marriage. "Greg was never mean," she recalls. "But all of a sudden we were fighting all the time. I had a gut feeling that there was more to his anger, and I was right."

It was on Memorial Day weekend that things came to a head. *"It was a Saturday and I had lunch ready for Greg. I called him and he wasn't where he was supposed to be. He came home very late and we had a huge fight. He left the house to go to a sports banquet and I ended up sleeping in the other room that night. That Sunday morning, I got up early and went to the beach to watch the sunrise. I prayed, 'Father, give me a sign. Am I being paranoid? Am I over-reacting?'"* In the meantime, Greg awoke and thought Ginny had gone to church. Attempting to smooth things over, he went to church. Something in the sermon that morning touched him to the core. He began praying and crying, and by the time he got home, he had made the decision to try to save his marriage.

In the meantime, Ginny had picked up his cell phone and noticed a number she didn't recognize. *"I dialed Star 67 and it was her voice mail. I freaked out. I told him I was leaving him. He begged me to believe him that nothing physical had happened between them; that it was just a friendship that had gotten out of control. I left the house and drove to a gas station and sat there sobbing. I tried to go to her house, but she lives in a gated community and I couldn't get in."* Ginny went home and, after a day spent fighting with Greg, she suddenly saw a change come over him.

"I watched him absolutely fall apart as he sat on the couch. It was as if he was suddenly seeing himself through my eyes as I forced him to look at what was happening to his life. He was filled with remorse and he promised never to see her again. The next day, I met with her and she told me the same thing – that theirs had not been a physical affair. I forced myself to believe them, although there was a seed of doubt even then."

During the following year, Greg and Ginny worked on rebuilding their marriage. They began focusing on putting God first and attended church regularly together. *"Greg was being great – loving and kind again – and we decided it was time to start a family. We had our baby girl and Greg was a great father and husband, but there was still doubt in the back of my mind that kept coming back. I kept pushing it from my mind, but once in a while I'd ask him again if he had sex with her, and he'd always deny it."*

Ginny prayed to God to allow her to get over this doubt, but it never left her. *"There was just a knowing deep inside of me, and it wouldn't go away. Each time he denied it, my trust for him got weaker."* One night, when Greg was playing with the baby, Ginny begged him again to *tell her the truth. "I know you had sex with her," she said. "I need to hear it from you. We can't go on living this lie. We can't heal unless you speak the truth."*

That night, Greg confessed that he had been lying to Ginny for over a year. Even though he had stopped the relationship on Memorial Day Weekend, his lies had come back to haunt him. Once again, he was about to lose Ginny.

When Ginny shared her grief with the pastor at church, he sent her to Don and Anne for ministry. Greg and Ginny began seeing Don and Anne regularly and, little by little, they learned how empty their marriage had been without Christ in the center. As they received ministry and joined with one another in prayer, Ginny was led to see that what had happened to Greg was between him and God. Greg had hit bottom in every part of his life. He had been the baseball star, the perfect husband, the perfect dad, the likeable guy who worked out but didn't use steroids, the handsome athlete who could do no wrong – and now, he saw that he had been a liar and a cheat. "God was telling him, "No, you're not perfect. I'm perfect. My Son is perfect." Greg was suddenly open to learning what being a Christian man is all about. It's based on truth.

"Don and Anne speak right into your heart," says Greg. "They know, through God, the right things to say and when to say them. I think their insights are divine."

Ginny and Greg are still working through the web of lies that nearly destroyed their marriage, but this time, they are relying on the healing power of God and the truth, no matter how painful. "I still feel like I have to know everything about Greg's affair," says Ginny, "and, sometimes, I still replay it all in my head. It's like a horror film that I can't stop watching. Greg knows I have to visually deal with this. Sometimes I ask him questions like, 'Who took whose clothes off?' and 'Were you standing or sitting? Who was on top when you had sex?' and 'Did you have oral sex?' – he answers whatever I ask. Over time, I've accepted the fact that my husband slept with another woman. I can picture it in my head. In spite of the pain, for me, it is important to know all the details so that I can eventually heal."

Comparing it to a Lifetime TV movie where the husband is cheating on his wife and you think, "That jerk. Don't believe him. He's lying," Ginny still has moments when she cries because her wonderful man was once that jerk who cheated on his wife.

"The husband I have now is like a husband I could never have dreamed of. It's amazing what God has done with him. We pray aloud every night. We focus on God. He even has someone come to his work and do devotions. He's a changed man, and I see God's hand in all of this."

"It was only when I was dead honest and at rock bottom that I found God," says Greg. "Now, there's a fire in me. It was always baseball first, then family, then God, but now I've seen that everything crumbles without Him first. Ginny and I had something special together and I know we'll have it again, but this time it will be with God in the center and better than anything we could have imagined. There's nobody on this planet that can give me what she gives me and I'll continue to answer her questions honestly and love her with the unselfish love I've never had before. The biggest surprise in all this is that now I know God is alive in me. I'm not doing what I do for myself or for Ginny, but for Him. I wish now that I could go back and play baseball for God. It's ironic. When God is in the center, everything else falls into place. Today, for the first time in my life, I'm batting 1000."

Seven years later (with the 2nd Edition of Sailing the Seven C's) Greg gave us an update: "Our cup is truly overflowing. Even a year or two ago, we'd never have thought things could get any better, but they are – as we draw closer to Christ, we draw closer to one another. There's no more 50/50 in our marriage – it is all 100/ 100 – totally unconditional love for both of us. That grace that Don and Anne talked about ... I'm the beneficiary of the grace my wife showed me and it completely transformed my life. I look at our two daughters, ages 7 and 10, and I see Christ in them. I tell Ginny, 'If you had turned your back on me, they wouldn't be here.'" Greg's life today is better than hitting a homerun in the World Series. He wins the earthly game of life every day.

Crying in Church

The sermon that Sunday was a powerful one dealing with relationships. As the pastor returned to the pulpit to pick up his Bible following the service, he noticed a young couple in a corner pew quietly sobbing. Jim and Joanna had been deeply touched by his sermon that day. They knew they needed God's help if their relationship was to survive. "You might want to call Don and Anne Bloch," suggested the Pastor gently.

Jim and Joanna had been through a lot in their short time together. "I am an alcoholic," admits Jim. "I came from a hideous childhood – a broken, fatherless home. I'd been in a drunken haze for ten years when I met Joanna. After we started living together, I still drank and partied with friends. I loved her, but not as much as I loved booze. We yelled at one another all the time and fought constantly."

"It wasn't all Jim's fault," says Joanna. "I was a control-freak. Whenever things didn't go my way, I put up a wall. I knew Jim was a good man. He was amazingly generous and loving sometimes, but if he crossed me in any way, I instantly judged him and put him down. I thought I knew all the answers. I was right and he was wrong. Our lives were full of conflict."

When Joanna became pregnant, Jim promised to change. "I couldn't imagine wondering what my kid was going to be like," he says. "I was not going to condemn my child to a life like mine. Joanna and I started talking marriage and even began looking for a church to attend. We both wanted to have God in our lives."

But a few months later, Jim got drunk after work, got in his car to drive home, and woke up in jail. "I didn't know how I got there," he recalls. "I was so angry at myself. What if I'd hit a kid and become a murderer that night? What if my kid had a dad in jail? That was a turning point for me."

Shortly after their daughter, Emma, was born, Jim and Joanna were married. "Emma was God's angel that He sent to us as a gift," says Jim. "We made vows to one another and vows to her the day we were married." Although Jim was no longer drinking, he and Joanna still continued to fight daily.

Their marriage was on the rocks that day they sat crying in church, while baby Emma waited for them in the nursery.

"Don and Anne hugged us," recalls Joanna. "They were like a spiritual Mom and Dad.

They taught us to look at one another and see Jesus. They asked us if we would verbally abuse Jesus like we did one another. They taught me to release control and allow Jesus to enter my life. They helped us open our hearts and let Him in. Our lives became centered in Christ and we were blessed like neither of us had ever been blessed before."

When life handed them the next conflict, the couple was to discover the true meaning of having Jesus in their lives. Joanna's pregnancy with their second child, Mary, was plagued with Hyperemesis-Gravidaren – a condition that afflicts 1 in 200 pregnant women, causing extremely severe nausea and violent vomiting. "I was desperately ill for nine weeks and lost my job," she recalls. "We couldn't pay our rent and the bills were piling up. Jim was working double shifts. It was very hard. We prayed and prayed."

One day, a neighbor knocked on the door. "I've seen you two at my church," he said, "and I've heard you have trouble. Our men's group at church voted to pay your rent and help with your bills until you're back on your feet." God answered their prayers. "He wants to take care of us," marvels Joanna. "All we have to do is give Him control of our lives."

Today, Jim and Joanna are sailing the seven seas C's of matrimony with confidence because they have Christ at the helm.

Faithful and True

My name is David, and this is my story.

Walking into our church on that Wednesday morning, I thought that this was probably it. Our marriage was over. Betty had found out that I was seeing another woman for the second time in three months. Even though we hadn't been attending church regularly, I had called our pastor for guidance and he asked me to call Don and Anne Bloch, the marriage counselors at our church. I called Don and set up a meeting for Betty and me to meet with him and his wife Anne. Betty and I were separated at the time and we met at the church. When I walked into the Bloch's office at the church Betty was there sitting with Anne listening to the song we picked out for our first dance at our wedding. She would not look at me, and I was expecting the worst. I had crushed her heart, Betty was very hurt and so was I. I couldn't understand how I could hurt the love of my life like this. We were both broken emotionally and spiritually. As we shared our story with Don and Anne, they assured us if we were willing to put hard work and commitment into saving our marriage we could have an even stronger marriage than we had before.

Sharing with Don and Anne my addiction with alcohol and porn and my past, Don referred me to a ministry called "Faithful and True" for men with sex addictions. It is a Christian based ministry for men all around our area. I started to attend meetings and found other men there with the same problems that I have that were healing. We also found that they have a ministry for spouses of men with sex addictions and Betty started attending these meetings. This has helped her a lot as well. I am forever grateful to Don and Anne for guiding us to this group.

With Don and Anne's help, we started communicating to each other our true feelings without arguments and loud voices. I moved back into our home and we started praying together and became members of our church. We have a goal to have our marriage Christ-centered, not self-centered. Our lives have truly changed. We still have a way to go and still have problems to deal with, but with Don and Anne's guidance we believe we will have a stronger marriage.

Exodus 10:2 NKJV
Tell your children the mighty things I have done.

The Battle is Over

It's not enough to escape your negative past. Rather, its power over you must be broken, otherwise it will chase you for the rest of your life. When you break away from something that keeps trying to recapture you it's crucial to get victory over it – otherwise you can't move forward and enjoy the blessing God has in mind for you. It's jarring to think something is over only to find it isn't. But remember, it was God who permitted Pharaoh to pursue the Israelites all the way to the Red Sea. Why? For two reasons: first "...that I may show [you] these signs of Mine..." (Exodus 10:1 NKJV) God wants you to see that when you put your trust in Him, obstacles and opposition mean nothing. He wants this experience to be a "landmark memory" you draw faith from when you face your next problem. Second, "...that you may tell.. [your children]... the mighty things I have done..." (Exodus 10:2 NKJV) You don't have to live under Pharoah (Satan's rule) any more. Like the Passover, when the blood of Jesus was applied by faith to the doorposts of your heart, your status changed. You're no longer a slave, but a child of God. The generational curse is broken. Your children can now grow up under God's blessing. Abuse, alcoholism. anger and abandonment may have been the story of your past, but it's no longer the truth about your future.

God can solve your problem in different ways, but sometimes He takes you through the Red Sea so that when you get to the other side you can look back and see Pharoah and his armies "dead on the seashore," (Exodus 14:30 NKJV) and know the battle is over!

Philippians 2: 3-4:
Do nothing out of selfish ambition or vain conceit, but in humility consider others better than yourselves. Each of you should look not only to your own interests, but also to the interests of others.

A sign in front of an old country church read: *Pain is inevitable – misery is optional.* We believe the word; "conflict" can be substituted for the word, "pain." *Conflict is inevitable – misery is optional.* Conflict *will* occur. It is as inevitable in marriage as it is in life.

We generally learn how to handle conflict the same way we learned communication skills - by observing and learning from our parents or caregivers. What did you observe as a child about resolving conflict? Before you put yourself in the victim role or have a pity party, understand that you *can* decide today that you are going to break old negative habits and learn new and healthier ways to resolve conflict. With God's help, you can change the way you respond to conflict.

The "Ostrich Syndrome"

One way of dealing with conflict is known as the "ostrich syndrome." We attempt to convince ourselves that if we ignore the conflict, it will go away in time. It never completely disappears; it clings to us. Even though time may lessen the sting, it does not always (as the saying goes) "heal all wounds."

Burying conflict and pretending it is not there is similar to throwing our garbage into a trashcan and placing a tight lid upon it. One hundred percent of the time, the accumulation will begin to ferment and build up putrid poisonous gasses. At some point, there will be a loud explosion and the lid will blow off. Someone may even get hurt in the process of the flying lid!

This is exactly what happens to us when we keep stuffing our conflicts into our hearts. Eventually, an explosion of anger, resentment, bitterness and even rage can occur. This will usually become an attack upon the one we promised to love and honor. Of course, there are some who "kick the dog", but the attack is most often against the one who disagrees with us. We then go into one of three modes so aptly described as *"fight, flight or freeze!"*

Unless you are a trial attorney, you probably do not enjoy conflict. Very few of us really do. We usually tend to avoid it at almost any cost. Sometimes, the aversion to conflict is so strong that it can nearly paralyze you. The first line of defense is to avoid it and attempt to pretend it does not exist. This pretense is temporary. The conflict will persist, so the best policy is to *face* it and seek an equitable solution.

A quote from Michele Weiner Davis' book, *The Divorce Remedy,* states: "People in loving marriages understand that conflict goes with the marital territory. It's more than unavoidable - it's necessary. The fact is, the single best predictor of divorce is the constant avoidance of conflict."

The Silent Treatment

A similar method of dealing with conflict is known as "The silent treatment." When using this method, we try to convince ourselves that to avoid conflict we'll just not talk about it. Then it will eventually resolve itself. Wrong! This build-up can cause deep depression if not resolved. One of you may show your anger toward your spouse by using "the silent treatment."

(Anne): I still remember the day in Kentucky when I thought a serious conflict was about to erupt in our early-married life. Don and I had only been married about seven months. It was a warm, sunny late spring day when I asked Don if I could help him by tilling our newly created fruit and vegetable garden. I so wanted to impress him by tilling every pesky weed! With his affirmative response, I was off to our special half-acre garden across the creek on our acreage. I felt so much joy participating with my beloved husband in creating our first garden together! Being somewhat of a perfectionist, I tilled each row several times.

As I stopped the tractor and looked back to admire my long labor-of-love, I could no longer see the cantaloupe plants that emerged from the hills Don had planted several weeks ago. I feared I had created a *major* conflict between us and feared even more what his reaction would be! After fighting back the tears and attempting to deal with my own emotions, I knew I had to tell Don that his prized cantaloupe production had been wiped out – by me.

My entire past of rejection went through my mind. My childhood experiences convinced me I would be unmercifully reprimanded and punished. My first and second husbands abused me verbally and physically when they lost their tempers. After getting up enough courage, I went to the house to explain to Don what had occurred in our garden. Don did not say a word.

He got up from what he was doing at the time and left the house!

This time there would be no verbal or physical abuse. Instead, it would be the silent treatment – another form of abuse that was quite familiar to me. I remembered past incidences when my second husband would live in a separate part of the house for several days or even weeks not talking to me without telling me why. When Don left the house I assumed this was going to be more of the same. What a way to begin a new marriage!

After what seemed like hours, Don came back into the house. He held out his hand, taking my hand in his and escorting me silently across the creek to the "crime scene." To my amazement, I saw several stakes in the ground where the cantaloupe hills had been a short time before. Don had placed a sign on top of each stake with "CANTALOUPE" written on it and an arrow pointing to the ground. He squeezed my hand, smiled and then hugged me tenderly.

Don had simply gone to the store, purchased more cantaloupe seeds, replanted them and marked them clearly. This was the solution to what I perceived would be a "stormy" conflict! I learned so much about my beloved Don that day. I learned about unconditional love, forgiveness and God's grace. What a precious memory!

Fight

Fight: leads to raising their voices ... which leads to fighting ... which leads to a winner and a loser. The winner feels superior. The loser feels controlled and devalued.

Flight

Just run away.

Freeze

"I am definitely a freezer," says Anne. "If there is conflict or a quick decision to be made, I literally freeze where I am, put my hands on my head, start to stutter, and can't even think. Don is very patient with me. With his hand on my shoulder, he keeps telling me to calm down. God is in control. It works every time. We always end with a hug.

Conflict Resolution

Knowing that conflict will eventually raise its head in your marriage, it is important that you implement a plan to deal with it. Learn to handle conflict in such a way that it will make a positive and permanent difference in your relationship. Many marriage therapists have written their own "Steps to Conflict Resolution." All are similar and all will work! It is up to you to use these helpful tools.

For instance, Dennis B. Guernsey's book, *The Family Covenant*, lists a powerful seven step "Litany of Conflict" based on Ephesians 4: 15 – 32.

Speak the truth in love. (Verse 15: *Instead, speak the truth in love, we will in all things grow up into Him who is the Head; that is Christ.*)

When the truth is spoken it often provokes anger. Handle that anger daily. Satan takes advantage if you let anger build. (Verse 26: *In your anger do not sin. Do not let the sun go down while you are still angry, and do not give the devil a foothold.*)

When you speak the truth, do so for the purpose of building up and edifying your relationship with the other person rather than tearing it down. (Verse 29b: *Do not let any unwholesome talk come out of your mouths, but only what is helpful for building others up according to their needs, that it may benefit those who listen*).

When you speak, do so at the appropriate time and place – that is, as it fits the occasion. (Verse 29c: see above verse).

Speak in such a way that you can imagine your statements being used for good in the other's life. That it may impart grace to those who hear. (Verse 29d: see above verse).

Don't let the power of negative emotions control you. (Verse 31: *Get rid of all bitterness, rage and anger, brawling and slander, along with every form of malice*).

Rather, be ruled by positive and constructive motives toward the other person. (Verse 32: *Be kind and compassionate to one another, forgiving one another, just as God, through Christ, forgave you*).

99

Pray. The first step is for both of you to pray together for God's guidance and wisdom for dealing with the conflict between you. Pray about a specific time to meet together and talk about the conflict. Seek His words and ask that great question, *"What would Jesus do?"* and *"What would Jesus have us do?"*

Schedule a Special Time Together

After you have prayed and found a good time for the two of you to meet objectively to deal with the conflict, make the commitment to do so. It is amazing how conflict will often pop up just before going to bed at night. Do not allow Satan to destroy what God may want for a time of intimacy. This is also a time when one or both of you are tired – not an opportune time for conflict resolution. However, it is crucial that you *do* decide on a time to work on the specific issue. To tell your spouse we will deal with this sometime "in the future" is really saying, "This is not important … you're not important." This invalidates the one who needs to talk. It *is* important to one of you, so deal with it at a specified time and place. Deal with the issue, not generalities.

Write it Down

Write down the details of how each of you contributed to the problem in the first place. Generally, you will discover that you have also played a role in the issue at hand. Remember, in this step, you concentrate on your contribution and not that of your spouse. This includes avoiding attack of your spouse or your spouse's family. Remember from communication skills that you use "I" statements rather than the accusatory "you" statements!

Now, make a list of your thoughts for possible solutions to the conflict, and be willing to compromise. Honor each idea, thought and feeling of your spouse as each of you share your list aloud. This is a time to work together and review each idea, whether or not you agree with it. "That's a dumb idea" or "That won't work" are not productive responses. Write down every suggestion. Always ask yourself, "Is what I'm about to say edifying my spouse?" Use the K.I.S.S. approach: "KEEP IT SIMPLE, SWEETHEART."

Next, discuss the merits of each potential solution suggested and select one that you are both willing to put into action. This is a time when your negotiation skills can come into play. It is also the time to honor one another in deciding how you will each contribute to making this work. Be specific, and again, be willing to compromise.

The Blame Game

Remember, in serious conflict resolution; do not allow "blame" to raise its ugly head. This is not about finding fault, rather about finding a loving solution. As long as one person blames the other, the accuser is not accepting responsibility for their part in the situation. By blaming others, we refuse to look at how we contributed to the problem. This will prevent us from making healthy changes in our own lives. DO NOT PLAY THE BLAME GAME!

Zero Through Ten

We have developed a tool we use whenever we have a decision to make. It goes a long way in eliminating arguments and hurt feelings. We call it "0 through 10". Whenever conflict arises regarding a decision that must be made, we discuss pros and cons of the possible outcome. After we are both satisfied that we have thoroughly shared our thoughts and feelings on the matter, we both think of a number from 0 to 10.

To choose zero (0), means "I absolutely do NOT think this is a good idea"; to select five (5) means "I really could go either way in this decision;" and to choose ten (10) means a robust YES!" Next step is to count to three. At the count of three, we both say out loud the number we have selected. We then add the numbers together. If they total 11 or more, we do "it." If 10 or less, we do not. In this way, we are BOTH participating in the decision-making process and assume a joint responsibility in solving the conflict. Also, it is the number that decides, taking pressure off of you.

This has worked for us with such minor decisions as selecting a movie or restaurant all the way to large financial purchases. It has also worked with countless couples that have come to see us with issues of conflict resolution. Try it. If you have children, remember that it is a fun and effective conflict resolution tool for all ages and all conflicts. It also works for making fun decisions.

Tangier

How we wish we'd had the "0 through 10" tool during the first two weeks of our marriage! Don won a trip to Spain, which is where we spent our honeymoon. We had an interesting experience that has caused us to refer to any similar situation today as a "Tangier." An all day sailing tour from Spain to Tangier was available on the second to last day of the trip. However, when we went to the boat's port of departure, we were informed that the sea was much too rough and we could come back the next morning when weather conditions would improve.

Neither of us *thought* the other wanted to take the trip. Therefore, we both *pretended* we did not wish to go. We later discovered that both of us desperately wanted to go, but because we lacked communication skills, lost out on an exciting adventure. We now caution one another not to have another "Tangier" as we sail on to our "0 through 10" decision-making tool. It has solved a lot of potential disappointments on our journey together. It has also taught us never ever to assume, and that there is no such thing as mind reading!

"B.T." (Before Tools)

While we are on the subject of mind reading, here is another "B.T." (Before Tools) incident that illustrates the importance of communication (or lack thereof):

(Anne): In 1981 I was recuperating from extensive, complicated surgery, which required bed-rest for two months. Don was absolutely incredible during this time! He did ALL the cooking, cleaning, shopping, laundry, yard work, which included my nine-hour weekly job of mowing the grass on our tractor, which I thoroughly enjoyed. He did all this on top of going to work at 4:00 AM five days a week.

Since our home was a tri-level and I was on the third floor he even set up a card table in one of the guest bedrooms so we could eat together. This, of course, required several trips from the bedroom to the kitchen. Not once did my precious Donny complain! He even spread blankets on the floor of our bedroom and invited our church fellowship group for a picnic so that I could see our friends. What a blessing! What unconditional, sacrificial love on my beloved Dons' part!

On the first day I was able to negotiate the stairs, I noticed that Don was getting ready to do laundry. Feeling guilty over my long convalescence and all that he had done for me, I immediately jumped in and started pushing all the buttons on the washing machine. To my amazement, Don threw the clothes on the floor and stomped out of the room. I was absolutely bewildered. What in the world was that all about??!

When we finally talked about it we revealed to one another our silent thoughts at the time of the incident.

Don's thoughts: *She thinks I don't even know how to do the laundry right; I have already set the dials.* (I did not know this.)

My thoughts: *Good Grief, I was only trying to help, what in the world just happened?* To quote Don, "It all came out in the wash."

Win-Win!

As you work toward your solution, affirm one another for working on resolving the conflict. Together, agree on a time within the week to discuss and evaluate your progress. If no solution is found, it is probably time to find a neutral outside person qualified to assist you.

When a solution is found, it is time to offer thanks and praise to God and to one another. It is time to celebrate your victory! There is a win-win solution in every conflict. It is hard work, and worth every bit of the effort you put forth. Through the above process and good communication skills, you will achieve the art of resolving conflict. Each time it will get easier until you find yourselves going through the process quite naturally.

The Bible is full of examples where our Lord used conflict to help his people grow. Examples: Joseph sold into slavery, Job, Noah, Abraham, Jonah, and Paul. Jesus began and ended his life on earth with conflict – a Virgin Mother giving birth in a lowly stable, King Herod's fury, Satan's temptations, Judas's betrayal, and His excruciating crucifixion. Gloriously, He was resurrected, took His rightful place in heaven, and lives today for all of us. The conflicts in marriage can also be resurrected. Conflict can be viewed with a defeatist attitude or as an opportunity for growth. The way it is handled makes all the difference in a relationship and in life.

Can you truly enjoy the spectacular view from the mountain if you've never been down in the valley? We cannot spend our lives on the beautiful mountaintop, where the air is thin and vegetation is scarce. The lush green growth occurs in the valley. Conflict is the valley that helps us to appreciate those breathtaking, but temporary ascents to the mountaintop. Each time we make it to the top of the mountain, we are allowed to see new mountaintops in the distance that beckon us. Only by traversing the valley can we hope to reach the next glorious mountaintop experience.

When connecting this concept with the Seven C's think of the recent movie *The Perfect Storm* and imagine what would have happened had Jesus stood in the center of that ship! Regardless of the intensity of the storm, or the depth of the conflict, your salvation lies within reach. Grab onto the life preserver named Jesus Christ!

Prayer of Salvation

Heavenly Father, I believe that Jesus Christ is your only begotten Son; that He became man, shed His blood and died on the cross to forgive my sins that were separating me from You. I believe that He rose from the dead to give me eternal life in heaven and abundant life in Him here on earth. Lord Jesus, I invite you to come into my heart. I receive you as my Lord and Savior. I confess my sins and ask you to cleanse me. I believe you are now living within me. Thank you, Jesus. In your name I pray.

CONFLICT
Ponder Page ...

1. What are some conflicts in your life? List them, and share the ways that you might individually deal with them. Discuss ways in which you may resolve them as a couple.

2. Is there anything in your past that causes you to avoid dealing with conflict?

3. Decide on the ground rules you will use in resolving conflict from now on.

Cost

Your cost is to give up the right to be right!
Learn to say the words "Please forgive me."
The cost of forgiveness is repentance.
Turn away from that which hurt your spouse.
Experience the joy of forgiveness and redemption.
Give control to Christ.
You'll find that your needs are met and exceeded.

Chapter Six

Cost
Defeating the Devil!

It was the day before Christmas in 1982 when Dr. Amy Norris, a prominent professor at a local university, made a desperate phone call to Don and Anne. "My husband of 33 years had left me for another woman. I was ready to toss everything overboard and drown in my sorrow. It was a time when families celebrate the birth of Christ, but I was alone and afraid. I had nowhere to turn, and then I remembered about this couple I'd heard about through a friend at the university."

Although Amy did not attend church regularly and had never met the Blochs, she called them. "I heard the desperation in her voice," says Anne. "Don and I went immediately to her home and prayed with her for two hours."

"I couldn't believe they'd come to me on Christmas Eve Day without even knowing me. They listened, they prayed, they helped me deal with my guilt, my sense of failure and my resentment," Amy said. She and her husband, Fred, a corporate executive, lived in a mansion in the best neighborhood in town and were prominent, popular citizens in the community. Her rise in academia and his in the corporate arena left little time in their lives for intimacy or communication with one another. Amy blamed herself for the break-up of their marriage. She was later to discover that sinister forces had crept into their lives while she and her husband were busy pursuing success in the secular world. Money was no object for this affluent couple, but when it came to paying the cost demanded in a Christian marriage, they were bankrupt.

"When I met Don and Anne, I was aware first of being enveloped in a great peace," Amy related. "That day, they showed me the true healing power of God." Through regular prayer and counseling with Don and Anne, Amy began to see the huge gap that had existed in her marriage. Her bitterness was replaced with forgiveness and her fear with certainty. She was suddenly armed with the strength of Christ within her as she prepared to do battle with Satan to save her marriage.

"We discovered, through many long hours of counseling with Amy, that the woman who had destroyed her marriage was truly a witch. She was a satanic high priestess in a coven who had set her sights on the wealthy businessman," says Anne. "It was not the first time we'd run into something so bizarre – in fact, the devil is very much a reality and he hates marriage – especially Christian marriages."

A year later, Anne sat in a tense courtroom and prayed as Amy conducted legal and spiritual battle with the woman who had literally bewitched her husband. "It was an amazing, yet not so uncommon, story of the devil at work in modern society. Without God in their lives, Amy and Fred were powerless."

Anne fixed her eyes on the woman in the witness stand and prayed continuously and silently in the Spirit. The elegant, arrogant woman began to get nervous, fidgeting and contradicting herself. "She lost her composure, lost the case and lost Amy's husband that day," grins Anne.

By Christmas 1983, the Norris's were together again, but this time with a new awareness of the cost involved in surviving an attack by the devil and the cost involved in preserving their new Christ-centered marriage. Today, they focus on loving one another and loving God. They minister to troubled couples in their church rather than focusing on working their way to the top. More successful than ever in the eyes of the secular world, Amy and Fred know now where their true riches lie. Understanding that their resources and social standing are gifts from God, they now use them for His glory. The Norris's are a powerful example of a couple nearly capsized by stormy seas who are now sailing on smooth waters.

"The Blochs saved my life," says Amy. "They helped me realize that Jesus had been standing at the door of our hearts, knocking and waiting for us to invite Him in. They brought Him right into our home, our hearts and into the center of our marriage. Through prayer, they rescued us from the talons of the devil. When you've been in the depths of the valley, the mountaintop is incredibly exciting. With Jesus firmly in the center of our marriage today, we are invincible."

Forgiveness Heals … Love Prevails

Helen was 23 years old when she married Jerry in December of 2000. She was looking for a stable relationship and Jerry, an "older man" with a six-year old son, filled that bill perfectly. Within a month of their marriage, a Jehovah's Witness knocked on their front door and Jerry politely invited him in. "Both of us were raised Catholic and when this young man began throwing all this information at us, we had so many questions that we called a friend who was a pastor and he led us to Christ that very night!"

They celebrated the New Year by joining CrossRoad Church and seeking God's guidance for meeting some of the challenges that faced them in their new marriage. Jerry's ex-wife was not in the picture at all, and being a workaholic, he had entrusted his parents with a great deal of responsibility in caring for his son. While Helen wanted to be a mom to Jerry's son, his family felt threatened by her. "There was a lot of toxicity in Jerry's family and I didn't understand it until much later," recalls Helen, "but our conflicts were about much more than parenting issues."

Each of them came to the marriage with some major baggage from the past … Helen's abortion at age 19 haunted her. Also, she harbored unforgiveness against her mother, who had mistreated her. Jerry's father had physically abused him at a young age, and he had seen his mother betray his father with another man, which led to jealousy and suspicion on Jerry's part. Jerry's jealousy and Helen's guilt combined with the challenges of raising a six year old with a new baby on the way led them to attend Don and Anne's Marriage on the Rock class.

"To this day, any time there is a marriage issue (and there are still many), we pray together about it and if we need to, we go to Don and Anne for ministry," says Helen. "It helps that Don and Anne have been through many of the same things. Anne and I both had nasty, mean, jealous moms and Don is, like Jerry, just so straightforward and matter-of-fact about what God has to say about things. However, there is a tenderness about Don that is a wonderful example for other men."

Helen and Jerry have been able to heal and forgive to the point where they feel confident in their marriage and have become close to their families on both sides, despite past hurts.

"Unforgiveness is so damaging, and blessing the people you love is so powerful," says Helen. "I can be so angry at Jerry, but the unconditional love I have for him through Jesus Christ trumps that anger every time. We wouldn't be together today if it weren't for the unconditional love Christ has for us. We model that love now, and as a result, we are raising three loving, warm, smart, giving children in a home very different from the ones in which we were raised."

Luke 9:23

[Jesus said] *If any man will come after me, let him deny himself, and take up his cross daily and follow me.*

Romans 8:13-14:

For if you live according to the sinful nature, you will die; but if by the Spirit you put to death the misdeeds of the body, you will live, because those who are led by the Spirit of God are sons of God.

Three times, Jesus said, *"Anyone who does not take up his cross and follow Me is not worthy of Me."* That is a powerful indictment. The sin of self-centeredness has taken center stage in the world today and is destroying marriages as well as relationships among families, friends and co-workers.

Paul refers to this sinful nature when he claims in Romans 8: 13-14, that by living for self only, you will surely die. This can be a physical, emotional or spiritual death. We submit to you that in our many years of pastoral ministry, we have observed that being self-centered will cause *death* to a marriage. That is why the C of Cost is one of the most dangerous. The huge waves in this C have sunk too many marriages. To die to self WILL bring life and blessings into your relationship!

A 2003 poll was conducted to find the average cost of a wedding today. Results showed that $22,000 per wedding was average – in 2014, that cost has nearly doubled! However, to our knowledge, there has never been a survey that measures the cost of *marriage!* That is what this chapter will address. Unfortunately, many couples have discovered the huge economical, emotional and spiritual cost that comes with divorce. Our desire is to give you the tools to prevent those devastating costs.

Have you ever felt like the salmon swimming upstream against the current? When you said those words at your wedding, *"I will,"* then jumped into the unknown waters upon returning from your honeymoon, did the current against you feel much stronger than you had anticipated?

Today's mindset often leads couples to live together prior to marriage. Perhaps, when everyday reality replaced the first glow of the wedding and honeymoon, you wished you had tried one of those "starter marriages." If you entertained those thoughts, let us remind you that the divorce rate is almost two-thirds higher for those who choose that stream. More importantly, it is sinning against God to live together before marriage.

The salmon fighting for its life to make it into calm waters for spawning is a vivid example of the cost of sacrificial love that comes with marriage. That sacrifice is necessary in order to reach God's living, refreshing waters of true intimacy with one another and with Him.

It has been our experience that there is a 100% success rate of all marriages when couples sail the seven C's with Christ at the helm. We have witnessed God's power of unconditional love and complete reconciliation. It matters not if there has been infidelity, emotional abuse or even physical abuse in a relationship when God turns it around for His glory. Unfortunately, there have been a few marriages that have chosen not to sail all seven C's. We dread watching helplessly as Satan scuttles Christian marriages that will end up on the bottom of the ocean floor. If you are having difficulties now, your marriage is worth fighting for. The consequences of NOT fighting for your marriage are much too costly.

Leave and Cleave

Let us now look into some of these costs of marriage. The first cost is leaving Mom and Dad to cleave to your spouse. At one time this was called, "Breaking the apron strings," and it can be a high cost to pay. Remember the symbolism of the unity candle explained earlier? The mothers light their candles at the beginning of the service. When the bride and groom light the center candle, the meaning takes on a different concept. After the center candle is lit, the new husband and wife extinguish the outside candles. This symbolizes the formation of a brand new family in the eyes of God. This does *not* dishonor the families of origin! Hopefully, we keep our fond memories of our parents and still have a special bond and relationship with them. What it is saying is that "one plus one equals one." God has created a *new* family and the bride takes the name of her new husband. Genesis 2:24 reminds us that a man will leave his mother and father and be united (cleave) with his wife and they will become one flesh. Jesus quotes the famous scripture in Matthew 19:5 and Mark 10:7. This is a huge cost to marriage that some husbands and wives are not willing to pay. Instead, they put their parent's needs over that of their spouse. Godly priorities are God first, spouse second, children third, extended family fourth, job and ministry fifth.

Forgiveness

To explain the second cost of marriage, turn back to the wedding homily at the beginning of this book and read once more the message from Pastor Dietrich Bonhoeffer found earlier in this book. This leads us into another cost of a Christian marriage – forgiveness.

As you read Bonhoeffer's words again, you will understand the costs involved in marriage. His guidance to "live together in forgiveness" is essential. He further states that forgiveness is *crucial* not only for marriage, but for *all* human relationships to survive.

An additional cost that comes through forgiveness is giving up the "blame game" as mentioned previously. Also, there is no more demanding "your *rights.*" Rather, you are to seek what *is right* through God's Word and in His eyes.

Forgiveness without repentance has been called cheap grace. In other words, repentance has to be part of the forgiveness bestowed upon us by our spouse. This is turning away from the things that physically, emotionally and spiritually wound your spouse. A grace-filled marriage allows for unity in the midst of diversity. A grace filled marriage will flow with forgiveness.

In a conversation we were blessed to have with Billy Graham, he told us, after 60 years of marriage to his wife, Ruth, he had discovered the one essential characteristic of a good marriage. It is a loving union between two forgivers. Ruth, when asked if she had ever considered divorce, answered "Divorce, no... murder, yes."

Changing "Me" to "We"

Another very high cost to a solid marriage is giving up self-centeredness. Before marriage many are wrapped up in "me." We are center stage in our lives and the world revolves around us. It's "my income, my car, my apartment, my accomplishments, me – me – me – mine – mine – mine." Marriage changes all that.

"Me" must change to "we."
"Mine" must change to "ours."
"Selfishness" must change to "selflessness."

If you plan on keeping separate checking accounts or even prenuptial agreements, your marriage may likely be a "Titanic" waiting to hit an iceberg. It is difficult to build trust and intimacy this way. Suspicions and doubts may eventually become part of your relationship. Things will appear as "yours" and "mine" rather than "ours."

Philippians 2: 3-5 gives us our guidelines to follow: *Do nothing out of selfish ambition or vain conceit, but in humility consider others better than yourselves. Each of you should look not only to your own interests, but to the interest of others as well. Your attitude should be the same as that of Christ Jesus.* We take the liberty to paraphrase this powerful scripture as it relates to marriage: "Do nothing out of selfish ambition or vain conceit, but in humility consider your spouse better than yourself. Your attitude toward your spouse should be the same as that of Christ Jesus."

Are you treating your spouse as you would Jesus? Is your attitude toward your spouse the same as it is toward Jesus? Do you realize that if Jesus resides in the heart of your spouse, every time you bring them shame or humiliation you are doing the same to your Savior? This is a terrible and huge price to pay for self-centeredness!

Throwing Darts

(Anne): I find the following story a remarkable example of how, so often, we do things throughout our lives without even realizing the impact we have created by thought, word or deed.

A seminary professor gave his class a special assignment. They were told to bring with them to class a photograph or sketch of a person in their lives with whom they had a poor relationship and unresolved issues. They were asked to think of those for whom they held unforgiveness and bitterness in their hearts. When the class met again, the professor collected the drawings and photos. Nothing else was said.

When the students entered class the following week, they found their assignment had been taped to the walls. At this point, the professor gave darts to the students, asking them to get in touch with their feelings toward each person who had wounded them and throw their darts at the appropriate picture.

After very enthusiastic throwing of the darts, they were asked to retrieve their drawings or photos. They were instructed to turn them over. The professor had placed a picture of Jesus Christ behind each one, illustrating the fact that when we throw darts at others, we are throwing darts at our Lord.

Is the picture of Jesus mentally on the back of the photograph of your spouse? When you speak to your spouse, do you do it as though you are speaking to your Savior? Do you treat your spouse the way you would treat Jesus? Do you honor your spouse as you do Christ?

If we continue to harbor resentments, expectations, unforgiveness or bitterness, happiness will surely dock elsewhere.

Put Christ First

The greatest commandment: Matthew 22:37-39. *Love the Lord your God with all your heart and with all your soul and with all your mind. This is the first and greatest commandment. And the second is like it: Love your neighbor as yourself.*

God is commanding us to first love Him with 100% of ourselves – Body, Mind and Spirit. He must come first. Jesus taught us to love our neighbor as ourselves. Your closest neighbor is your spouse.

At first, it may seem that the cost of handing over control to Christ is prohibitive. However, you will find that allowing Him to be the Captain on your voyage will eliminate the incredible expense of unrealized expectations. The only expectation each of you should have of the other is "to love God with all your heart, soul and mind, and to love your spouse as yourself."

You are in direct conflict with God when you physically, emotionally, verbally or spiritually abuse your spouse – and when you make unrealistic expectations or conditions upon your relationship. You cannot love with "conditions" or "expectations." You are to love your neighbor just as he or she is – unconditionally. One day you will meet Jesus face to face. What will your response be when He asks you, "Have you loved your spouse as I have loved you?"

With God first, and your neighbor (spouse) by your side, learn to put Jesus Christ in the center of your relationship. Ask, "What would Jesus do?" in every situation. Allow Him to be your compass at all times.

When Jesus is at the center of your marriage, His respect and unconditional acceptance is there for each of you. When you begin to die to self and allow Jesus to take control, your relationship will begin to heal. Respect, trust and unconditional acceptance are all prerequisites for confiding, which leads to true intimacy.

Your goal: To become so closely entwined with God and one another that the triangle becomes a dot! The triangle is one of the symbols Anne had engraved inside Don's wedding ring. It is a symbol that means intimacy in the truest sense of the word.

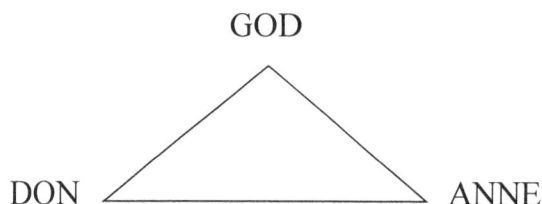

GOD

DON   ANNE

No "Quick Fix"

When wounded couples come to us for a "quick fix" for their relationship, we inform them that there is no such plan. God's plan is one of commitment, trust, respect and progress. The cost is paid on the installment plan – one of the few long-term deals guaranteed to reap a profit. For a wedding to turn into a marriage, the way God has intended, takes time and effort. It is a process. It can be hard work and there is definitely a cost, but the long-term benefits are heavenly. In fact, they are eternally awesome!

The problems of infidelity, addictions, unemployment, racial discrimination, in-law conflicts, incest and homosexuality are as old as time. Guilt from past mistakes, child-raising disagreements, fear of failure or fear of success, step-family problems, religious differences, weight problems and self-centeredness – these are universal. Righteous anger, misplaced blame, bitterness, indifference, incompatibility, boredom, resentment, jealousy and revenge have been part of the human condition since Adam and Eve ate of the tree of knowledge.

"I'm sorry" is only the first step. It MUST be followed with "Please forgive me." You are asking for God's forgiveness as well as that of your spouse. Finally, repentance: Turn away from what you have done and make a commitment to turn away permanently.

The cost of forgiveness and repentance will be repaid, one-hundredfold, as you will be blessed with tender intimacy in all areas of your relationship. Too often, there is the mindset of one spouse that says – "If you change, then I'll change! You make the effort first to show your sincerity!" With this mindset, there will be no change; only an outpouring of stubbornness. Much too often, the only one who benefits is the divorce attorney.

Obedience

Jesus calls us to obedience. It is through obedience to Him that blessings flow. This is a cost that you may feel is difficult to pay, but the investment returns are guaranteed! If we love Him, we will obey His commands. He commands us to love one another.

Of course, as we walk with Him, we will stumble along the way! God knows this about us! As long as there is evil in the world and we succumb to the darts of the evil one, we will fall. When we do, we have an all-powerful Savior who will be there for us. He will help us up on our feet, brush us off, and put us on His path once again!

Being a Child of God

To follow Jesus means to recognize and honor your spouse as a child of The King; to see one another through God's eyes and heart. It grieves God when one of His children is emotionally, physically, spiritually or verbally abused. When your spouse sheds tears of pain, Jesus is weeping also.

Being a Child of God does not merely mean to *know* or to *do*. It is not how much knowledge you have or how many Bible quotes you can come up with, or what you have done on God's behalf today. What is crucial to your journey is to *be*!

During one counseling session a husband and wife both said: "I'll start honoring you as a gift from God when you begin to honor me as a gift from God!" What an impasse that was! This is nothing but conditional love. "I'll love you if" or "I'll love you when ..."

What happens in many of these conditional relationships is that the husband finally recognizes his role as spiritual head of the family and repents of his behavior before God and his wife. He then begins to treat his wife with respect, with unconditional acceptance, and even blesses her each day. She is recognized as a child of God and treated as such.

Gradual Change

In some cases, there is no immediate response or change on behalf of the wife. A warning to husbands is not to fall into Satan's trap by believing the self-talk of "I did this for her and she didn't do anything in return! Therefore, I'll stop accepting her as a gift from God!"

In almost all instances, the spouse gradually begins to change when treated with love and respect. In rare instances, the change occurs immediately. The change of attitude may go something like this: "Wow! He's treating me like a queen! If I'm a queen, I'm going to begin treating him like a king!" Change will take place, especially when you're willing to take the initiative, without the expectation that the other will change first!

Remember, always, to sail the C of Compassion. Refer again to *Colossians 3:12 – 14*, which tells us: *Therefore, as God's chosen people, holy and dearly loved, clothe yourselves with compassion, kindness, humility, gentleness and patience. Bear with one another and forgive whatever grievances you may have against one another. Forgive as the Lord forgave you. And over all these virtues put on Love which binds them all together in perfect unity.*

(Don): In 1993, God spoke quite boldly to me. I wrote down what I believe He was telling me:

> **I invite you to death;**
> **I call you to die.**
> **I call you to die to pride...**
> **I call you to die to self...**
> **I call you to die to the world's image of success...**
> **I invite you to join Me in resurrection power.**
> **Surrender and follow Me.**

I share this with you because I believe it is what God calls all of us to do in marriage. I invite you to read it again and ask the Holy Spirit to reveal to you how this may apply to your life and your relationship with God and your spouse.

Let's look at II Timothy 3: 1 – 5. This is Paul's description of "Godlessness in the last days." If you feel you may be in the "last days" of your marriage, please heed Paul's warning and consider where you are in relation to his description.

But mark this: there will be terrible times in the last days. People will be lovers of themselves, lovers of money, boastful, proud, abusive, disobedient to their parents, ungrateful, unholy, without love, unforgiving, slanderous, without self-control, brutal, not lovers of the good, treacherous, rash, conceited, lovers of pleasure rather than lovers of God – having a form of godliness but denying its power. Have nothing to do with them.

Lovers of themselves.
This is being completely self-centered with no regard for others. (If it feels good, go for it! Just do it!)

Lovers of money.
Is financial wealth the ultimate goal of your journey on earth?

Boastful.
Does conversation need to revolve around you and your accomplishments?

Prideful.
Is pride blinding you to the reality that your gifts come from God?

Abusive.
Abuse comes in several different forms: verbal, spiritual, emotional, physical and sexual. They all can have devastating lasting effects.

Unforgiving.
Is unforgiveness eating away at your heart, killing you slowly from the inside?

Lacking self-control.
Are you presently struggling with addictions in order to hide pain? Is your sexual appetite or any other appetite out of control?

Lovers of pleasure rather than lovers of God.
Do you convince yourself you do not need Christian fellowship? Is Sunday merely a day to sleep in or chase a golf ball around the course, or do whatever pleases you on your "day off?"

Finally, Paul tells us to have nothing to do with people who possess these traits to which we need to die. Make a list of your friends. Use this checklist to review their character or character flaws. Do not allow them to attach to you and be careful of your association with them. Whom will you choose to serve – God or self? As you slowly die to the worldly view of self-centeredness, you will give up pursuing your happiness as an individual and begin to pursue happiness as a couple.

When we give control of the ship to Jesus, we can – and will – sail out of this treacherous C and reach the calm waters of a Godly marriage. Jesus Christ has to be our pilot and our navigator. He becomes our most powerful shield in overcoming shots across the bow. When we call upon Him as our "Captain," Jesus will respond to our invitation. He will take the helm and sail us into the spectacular C of Celebration!

COST
Ponder Page...

1. Are each of you willing to pay the cost of moving to selflessness? Is there anything standing in the way of your doing so?

2. Are you willing to accept the cost of giving up your right to be right in order to forgive and be forgiven? At this time, what steps will you take toward doing so?

3. When there are disagreements between you, are you willing to pay the cost of doing whatever it takes to reach a win-win conclusion? Can you think of a disagreement that was resolved recently? How did you do it?

4. Do you seek a healing of the past and make a difference; or do you remain a victim of the past and make excuses? Write about what needs healing and then seek help.

5. Review your list of friends as well as your own checklist.

6. Do you have any unresolved conflicts now that need resolution?

Celebration

God intended for all of life to be a celebration!

Hugging, touching, laughing, loving – celebrating!

On your wedding day, your heart overflows with joy.

With Christ at the helm, you are on the Love Boat!

Choose a permanent celebration cruise!

Chapter Seven

Celebration

Can These Bones Live?

Ezekiel 37, 1-6: The hand of the Lord was upon me, and he brought me out by the Spirit of the Lord, and set me in the middle of a valley; it was full of bones. He led me back and forth among them, and I saw a great many bones on the floor of the valley, bones that were very dry. He asked me, "Son of man, can these bones live?" I said, "O Sovereign Lord, you alone know." Then he said to me, "Prophesy to these bones, and say to them, 'Dry bones, hear the word of the Lord!' This is what the Sovereign Lord says to these bones: I will make breath enter you, and you will come to life. I will attach tendons to you and make flesh come upon you and cover you with skin; I will put breath in you, and you will come to life. Then you will know that I am the Lord.'"

When Mark, a Navy Officer, returned from a five-month deployment at sea, he was prepared for a great celebration! He had exciting news to share with his wife, Lana. "I'd been selected for a promotion to Commander! Our 17th wedding anniversary was coming up, we had two fine sons, and now, this promotion. I was on top of the world!"

Lana had news to share with Mark, as well. She wanted a divorce.

Mark's pleading and promises fell on deaf ears. Lana was not happy and shouldering the responsibility of home and family for months at a time while he was at sea was difficult. She missed her family back home. She had fallen out of love with Mark and just didn't care any more. Her mind was made up. She wanted out!

Four days before they were to celebrate their 17th wedding anniversary, Lana took the boys and went back to her hometown in the Midwest.

Within days, Mark had fallen from the top of the world into a valley of dry bones. "My family was gone, money had been divided, I felt like I'd lost everything. The house echoed. The loneliness was unbearable." Mark loved Lana a great deal but had neglected her needs.

Mark had never met Don and Anne, but had seen them in church and knew of their ministry. "Their faces beamed with God's love. I went to them for comfort." Mark wept in their arms as they prayed for him and for his marriage.

In the meantime, Lana had attended a church service in her hometown and had heard a moving sermon on marriage. "There is no coincidence," says Mark. "God was working His plan for both of us."

"Although I had never met Lana, I asked Mark's permission to call her," says Anne. "I told her, from my own experience, the hard truths of divorce and single-motherhood. I told her of the hurts that go beyond words. We then talked of the infinite joys of a Christ-centered marriage. We talked and prayed together for a very long time. Our prayers lit up the long distance lines!"

By the end of that anointed conversation, the healing of Mark and Lana's marriage had begun. Anne's words and prayers, combined with the sermon on marriage she had just heard began to make Lana reconsider her decision. She called Mark the next day to inform him she had decided that their marriage still might be saved. Mark continued to see Don and Anne. The telephone lines between Jacksonville and Lana's hometown continued to buzz as words and prayers were exchanged regularly. Weeks later, Lana and the boys returned to Jacksonville.

Lana discovered that she had a lot of anger over unmet needs. Mark discovered that he had been taking his family for granted. Together, they discovered that they needed Christ in the center of their marriage.

Eventually, Don and Anne officiated at the renewal of Mark and Lana's wedding vows. Their sons were ring bearers. It was the celebration Mark had longed for – and so much more. "Never doubt God's love for you and the way He shows His love by placing His people in your life just when you need them the most," says Mark. "I know He gives second chances. He truly breathes life into dry bones."

Philippians 4: 4-5: *Rejoice in the Lord always. I will say it again: Rejoice! Let your gentleness be known to all. The Lord is near.*

Psalm 118:24: *This is the day the Lord has made; Let us rejoice and be glad in it.*

(Don): Throughout the writing of this book, I have been awakened in the early hours of the morning with God compelling me to write. In the beginning, I would attempt to bargain with God, and advise Him that I was available at 7:00 a.m. as well. This was all to no avail, as I could not fall back to sleep unless I got up and wrote for one to two hours. Then sleep would fall gently. I would awaken refreshed, most probably because He finally convinced me to be obedient to His call.

You have undoubtedly observed in past chapters that the dictionary is my friend and I often seek man's definitions of words. This morning I had one of those "3 a.m. wake-up calls from God." He seemed to be saying to me – "Do not head for the dictionary on this one; I will give you **My** definition of "celebration." Just write this down:

"CELEBRATION IS THE DESSERT OF LIFE"

"Wow God, that's profound," was my only response. God saves the dessert for last, just as we do with our meals. Our dessert is usually the best part of the meal, and usually the reward we give our children when they have completed their meal. Perhaps it is God's reward to us, His children, for passing through the previous stormy C's. God does not want us to miss the Dessert of Life – our grand celebration with Him, through Him and for Him.

There are many avenues for spiritual growth. Many of them seem to center around celebration. This saves us from taking ourselves too seriously. This truly opens us and frees us to receive more of God's grace, which in turn brings His true peace and joy.

Ancient Celebrations

The ancient Israelites knew how to celebrate. God actually commanded them to do so. They did. The Seven Feasts are celebrated to this very day. God gave them these feasts, as recorded in Leviticus 23. For three of the Seven Feasts they were to go to Jerusalem to celebrate. This was indeed a hardship in Biblical times because of the challenges of travel. Yet they set off for the city of Zion in great anticipation of the joy ahead of them.

King David knew how to celebrate! What a joy and release it would be for us to acquire just a small portion of celebration from David into our own lives. We may, however, need to subdue it just a bit when it comes to dancing unclothed in the streets!

(II Samuel 6:14). David celebrated with joyous music and dancing; the inhibitions fell as he was visibly transformed by the power of God's love.

An entire town celebrated and rejoiced with blessings at the wedding of Ruth and Boaz. Through Ruth, celebrating is in the bloodline of David and on to Jesus. Spiritually, this same inheritance of celebration is passed on to us as believers in our Savior.

How about the celebration of Esther and Mordecai when they witnessed the destruction of the evil man, Haman, after he tried to annihilate the Jews? A great celebration throughout the land took place. In fact, this Jewish holiday called Purim is still celebrated with pomp and joy every spring with special food, games and clowns (Esther 7).

These are only a few of the stories of joyous celebration throughout Scripture. There certainly are many more, including the prophet Isaiah prophesying over the celebration in Zion and King Hezekiah celebrating over the cleansing of the temple prior to the Passover. What a celebration of joy this was, as recorded in II Chronicles 29 and 30! It is described as "singing to the Lord accompanied by trumpets and the instruments of David, King of Israel. The whole assembly bowed in worship while the singers sang and the trumpeters played." How exciting it is to witness this same celebration in some churches today, where God is praised in spirit-filled, joyous worship.

Isaiah 61 is one of the prophecies of the coming ministry of Jesus. Isaiah claims He will come to bind up the broken hearted, proclaim freedom for the captives (meaning emotional, spiritual and physical freedom), proclaim the year of the Lord's favor (celebration of Jubilee), comfort all who mourn and grieve, bestow on the people a crown of beauty rather than ashes, oil of gladness instead of mourning, and a garment of praise instead of a spirit of despair.

In Luke's gospel in chapter four, we read that Jesus went into the synagogue in Nazareth, unrolled the scriptures and read this exact passage of Isaiah. Upon completion, He announced that on this very day this scripture has been fulfilled! What a proclamation! The joy and ministry of Jesus is available for all.

Your Wedding Celebration

Do you remember the celebration that took place on your wedding day or at the last wedding you attended? In Jesus' day, wedding celebrations were awesome. Usually the entire village would participate, not only in the wedding service, but also in the torchlight parades at night. The bride and groom wore attire similar to a king and queen, and the wedding celebration usually lasted a week. With the cost of a wedding today, we can be thankful weddings no longer last that long! However, the royal aspect is still possible. Wouldn't it be fabulous if husbands treated their wives like a queen, and wives treated their husbands like a king! That needs to be the goal of every married couple. Even when children join the family, it should be remembered that the family is not a "democracy" where majority rules, rather, a beloved "monarchy."

A Wedding Ring … Lost in the Dead Sea

(Anne): We were in Israel in 1981 with Rev. Terry Fullam and his wife, Ruth. Terry is a famous Episcopal Priest from Connecticut. It was about him that the book, *Miracle in Darien*, was written. On the next to last day of our adventure, we were going to swim in the Dead Sea. We were told we absolutely must take off all our rings because we would shrink the minute we entered the water and our rings would slip off. People who weren't going in the water were holding jewelry for those of us who went in. Don said, "I am never going to take off my wedding ring." While we bobbed around in that "unsinkable" salt sea, Don was on shore taking photographs.

The rocks were large and slippery along the shore. As I watched Don enter the water, he slipped on the rocks. He had an awful grimace on his face. My first thought was that he had hurt himself. I reached him only to discover that he had lost his wedding ring almost the minute he hit the water. We all looked for his ring, but had to leave for the Masada without finding it. Don was very quiet on the bus ride to the Masada and back to the hotel. He was so upset that he had lost his wedding ring that he didn't stay to visit with people in the lobby. He went right up to our room and to bed.

Being dyslexic, with no sense of direction, I got lost on the way to our room and wandered past a jewelry shop. In the window was a wedding band on which there was

Hebrew engraving. That was especially significant because when we had visited the Holocaust Memorial, Don had gotten teary. He'd lost part of his family in the Holocaust and as we were leaving the museum, he said, "I've just been with my family and I don't want to leave them." Here was a wedding ring with Hebrew writing that I knew would mean so much to Don! I went in the shop and told the lady the story of how Don had lost his wedding ring and I wanted to buy this one. She said it was a sample and not for sale. I was so disappointed. My hand was on the door to leave her shop when she said, "I don't know why I'm doing this, but I will sell you this ring (which, by the way, was the perfect size for Don). I went back to the counter and began writing a check. She said, "I'm sorry, I can't take personal checks." I was afraid to give her our credit card because I didn't know where we stood financially at the end of this trip. I gave her a big hug and told her how awesome it was that she had been willing to sell me the ring. Again, with my hand on the door, I heard, "I don't know why I'm doing this either," she said, "but I will take your personal check." I was so grateful, excited and appreciative.

The Hebrew words on Don's new ring were from the Song of Solomon: "I am to my beloved as my beloved is to me." I did not tell Don about the ring. We were on the bus to the Tel Aviv Airport, where Terry Fullam announced to our group that Don and I were going to have a renewal of our vows with Don's new wedding ring! Don was dumbfounded. People gathered around who weren't even in our group as we were doing our vows. Our flight was at Gate 7 – the number of completion! God is amazing!

Terry had asked me to give my testimony at the Garden Tomb. After my testimony and our vows, Don took my face in his hands and said, "Anne, you will never be rejected again." There were many hearts touched by Don's gesture of love and assurance. Many tears were shed. When we got on the plane, members of the group wrote out a wedding certificate and everyone signed it.

Since then, at the 50th anniversary celebration of Israel being a state, Don bought me a wedding band from Israel that matches his. And now, the rest of the story … early in 2012, I was washing dishes at CrossRoad Church when my friend turned on the garbage disposal and we heard a clang, clang, clang … it was my wedding ring! Precious Ben Fleming spent a day searching for the ring, but to no avail. My wedding ring was lost. On our 35th Wedding Anniversary, October 29, 2012, Don presented me with a new wedding ring ordered from Israel, made by the same man who made the other. Our dear friend Pastor George Spencer, head of Pastoral Care at CrossRoad Church blessed it for us. On our 40th, we shall again renew our vows. What a glorious celebration that will be!

Don's Dead Sea disaster turned out to be a blessing in disguise … a beautiful renewal of our marriage covenant … again and again. Each time I look at our lovely rings, I smile at the way God works!

Saving the Best for Last

In Luke 15, Jesus told a story of a great celebration, when the prodigal son came home to his father. The father prepared a great feast to celebrate the return of his lost son. Recall for a moment the gifts the father gave to his son. He first clothed him with a robe that was a sign of honor. He then gave his son a ring that represents authority. Similar to a wedding ring, it may have meant a commitment to his son. Finally the young lad received sandals – the symbol of freedom. Only slaves were barefoot. (The slaves in our nation's past knew scripture well and sang a spiritual song called, "All God's Chillun Got Shoes.") The older son, full of resentment, bitterness, and unforgiveness, missed out on the celebration. Don't you miss out!

Let us recall, also, when our Savior commemorated The Last Supper. He was obeying God's command to celebrate the Passover every year. The Jewish people still celebrate the Passover annually for their freedom from slavery and oppression from the hands of the Egyptians. We as Christians are called to celebrate the Lord's Supper as *our* freedom from the slavery and oppression of sin and death.

It is no coincidence that Jesus' first miracle took place during a wedding celebration in Cana (John 2:1-11). When Jesus shows up, the party gets exciting! This will happen in your own lives when you invite Jesus into your life and especially into your marriage. Jesus loved celebrations. He grew up in a devout Jewish family celebrating all the feasts of Israel. Celebration was part of His heritage, and that heritage now belongs to us.

There was a mid-eastern belief that wine was essential at wedding celebrations. If wine was not present, this would bring humiliation to the host. It was the custom to begin the wedding feast with the best wine. After the guests were fully "rejoicing" with food, wine and dancing, the host could switch to some less expensive wines kept in storage.

Jesus came to the rescue of the wedding host who had run out of wine. He turned gallons of water into the best wine! An old rabbinical saying was – "Without wine there is no joy." Today, that can be translated to "Without *Jesus* there is no joy."

In the miracle at Cana, Jesus made certain that the best wine came last. In our own relationship, the best is yet to come as we await that glorious moment of celebration when we dine with our Lord at His Heavenly banquet table. Until that time, God calls us to keep the celebration going here on earth. The best comes last: No wonder God refers to *Celebration* as ***THE DESSERT OF LIFE!***

Celebrate Now!

Too often, Christians see salvation only in terms of eternal life. Jesus made it very clear "The Kingdom of God is at hand." We can and should take part in Kingdom living here on earth. If you believe you will just get by and receive your reward in heaven, you are missing the boat! There are incredible rewards here on earth. One of the greatest rewards is seeing your marriage relationship as part of Kingdom living in the present.

Celebration is an option for all of us. It is a gift from God that some choose to accept, while others do not. Many people with whom we have ministered over the years have never learned to celebrate due to an oppressive childhood. The victim role is one that we must release in order to enjoy and celebrate life. If you've never learned to celebrate, this may be the time to recreate your lost childhood and learn how to play. Jesus calls us to come to Him as little children.

A Little Child Will Lead Us

We recall several people who have come to see us for ministry with broken childhood dreams and did not know how to play as a child. We usually had such things as puzzles, games, pick up sticks and etch-a-sketch available in our office for such times. There were people who felt too uncomfortable to sit on the floor and play games. It took time to build trust before they could "let themselves go" with childlike faith. We can, indeed, recreate our childhood through play. What was it in your childhood that gave you great joy? Or what was missing in your childhood? Talk about these things with your spouse. There is a little child in each of us longing to emerge, and it is never too late.

Anne had a lost childhood and needed help recreating this treasure. Today she plays with a childlike wonder that is contagious.

(Anne): In the 1970's, our dear friend and mentor, Dr. Francis MacNutt, with whom we were in ministry for many years, mentioned that I needed to create a childhood I never had. I had absolutely no idea how to even begin.

My precious Don began the process by bringing me a new toy each week. I still have a wonderful collection of tinker toys, coloring books with huge crayons, Etch-a-Sketch, puzzles, jacks, pick-up sticks and various other games.

It is difficult to admit, but the "child" in me became so totally frustrated because I could not learn the jacks, that I hid them. Then the "adult" in me blamed it on dyslexia. The jacks are still hidden, because now the "senior" me can't remember where they are!

The competitive spirit within me drove me to practice pick-up-sticks until I could almost become a professional. You would be amazed at the number of adults who were in such professional fields as doctors, attorneys and clergy who really let their hair down playing this game with great gusto! At one time, a friend and her psychiatrist husband were our houseguests. She was thoroughly enjoying herself playing pickup-sticks. Unfortunately, he was uncomfortable and much too sophisticated to enjoy himself with the other adult children.

We had decided that my "playtime" would be in the evenings while Don was drawing plans for buildings, which he was selling at that time. He worked for a company that sold barns and stables. One day at 2:00 AM Don came downstairs where I was engaged in a puzzle, and suggested we put a time limit on my "playtime."

One evening, like a little child seeking daddy's approval, I went running upstairs with the unique design I had made on my etch-a-sketch. Don did a wonderful job of affirming both my design and me.

At the local Wal-Mart, there was a big sale on play-doh. I looked around to make certain no one was in sight. I turned into "Little Anne," looking up at Don with pleading eyes and a sweet little girl smile, rubbed his arm and said, "Oh, Donny, please may I have some play-doh?" The next thing we knew, a little girl went running up to her daddy with the same act. It worked for her, too! When we checked out, they were right behind us. Don turned to me in front of everyone and said, "Now, Anne, you may not play with your play-doh until all your toys are picked up." I wish you could have seen the facial expressions of those around us! I would really like to have known what they were thinking.

Don came downstairs one night while I was working on a jigsaw puzzle of the United States and he started putting pieces in the puzzle! Something rose up within me. Before I realized what was happening, these words came out of my mouth: "This is *my* puzzle and *I* want to put it together all by myself!" I even had my hands on my hips in a threatening stance. I was so embarrassed. Having been an only child living way out in the country where there were no other children with whom to play, I was not good at sharing. My best friends were my magnificent horses. It was very hard to share them, as they might love someone else more than they loved me. That would have crushed my heart.

Growing up, I was never allowed to even look like I was angry. Talking back or even being in opposition to someone was strictly forbidden. All of a sudden for the first time in my life, I knew it was safe to express myself without the fear of rejection. What freedom to know that Don would not withdraw his love from me because of my very inappropriate outburst! That moment was a great revelation for me. It is difficult to put into words the tremendous joy, peace, grace, trust and true love I have felt every day with Don throughout our 37 years of marriage!

In Madison, Indiana, where Don and I attended church, we were invited to give a presentation to a Marriage Encounter reunion group. I worked very hard in preparation for the event. Upon arrival at the church, I was totally caught off guard to find a surprise party for my 50th birthday! Our dear friends Sally and Hank Murray even drove down from Michigan to celebrate with us! I was presented with a huge hand-made toy box that had "Little Anne's Toys" painted on it, made by our dear friends Peg and Steve Nethery. The guests brought games of all kinds, stickers, coloring books, paint sets, stuffed animals and every kind of toy you can imagine as gifts to fill the toy box. I still have that beautiful gift of love. I think of that party and all those wonderful friends and family every time I pass the toy box, which is, incidentally, the envy of every child in the neighborhood. We even had it in our office at one of the churches where we ministered with children AND many adults in order to help them get in touch with their inner child.

At the birthday party, we played wonderful games such as "pin the halo on the angel," passing an orange from one team member to another under our chin, and a relay race balancing a ping-pong ball on a spoon carried in our mouth. I think we played every game ever invented for children. What was so exciting to all of us was the fact that, together, we were celebrating my renewed childhood as *a gift from God*!

Unfortunately, it was revealed that there were a couple of people in our group who were not free enough to enter into the celebration. My heart ached for them because they were fearful of letting themselves be childlike. I so much wanted them to just cut loose and have fun, without embarrassment. On a happier note, Marge, one of our senior citizens performed the Charleston for all of us. What a treat that was!

I also have the set of Children's Bible Stories that Don would read to me every evening. That was so incredibly special. We still get them out every once in a while to read aloud to one another and when our grandchildren visit. Now, in spite of dyslexia and a childhood of taunting because reading was difficult for me in first grade, I take great pleasure in reading daily devotionals to Don each morning. This is a wonderful healing for me and it is so meaningful that Don is part of my freedom! Likewise, it is important to share your childhood years with your spouse. Voids in your past can still be filled by your spouse if they know what those unmet needs are.

We plead with you to be very intentional about being free to be child-like with one another. Celebrate your childhood with one another, celebrate your adulthood with one another, celebrate your Lord together, celebrate your marriage to the fullest in every way, every day … to create a union of celebration. Learn to celebrate each day!

Celebrate Your Love

We tend to celebrate only birthdays and anniversaries. Generally, we give gifts on these days only, but we need to let our spouses know that they are a gift to us from God – every day. As husband and wife, make every effort to celebrate each week with a date night. This does not have to be an expensive evening dining out. It can be as simple as taking a walk together, watching a video, going to a movie, a concert, taking a bike ride, playing games or doing whatever you enjoy together.

Your wedding began with a celebration of great joy. Too many times we fall into the same old everyday rut of making a living instead of making a life after the bloom of the honeymoon is over. Reality sets in – daily routine sets in – the joy of courtship begins to wane. Problems at work infiltrate your home. This is the time to capture or recapture the pathway to celebration!

Celebration is the maintenance of a joyful attitude toward family and God. *Celebration* has been defined as true worship and adoration of a living and loving God. If you are blessed with children, it is crucial for the entire family to learn to celebrate life together. The Jewish expression – *"Le Chaim"* — usually given as a toast, means a loud *YES* TO LIFE!

If you place celebration on the back burner of your life, your marriage may only simmer and eventually burn out. Keep the flame burning by celebrating with a childlike joy and fun together. Do not allow Satan to interfere by putting business or busyness first in your routine. Do not allow conflict to get in the way. Agree to set aside a specific time to deal with any issues that arise. Brainstorm new ways to have fun as a couple. Write down some suggestions, place in a "fun" jar and pick one. Then *JUST DO IT!*

Your attitude usually determines whether or not you will celebrate together. Your attitude will also affect *how* you celebrate. The following are some ways you can change your attitude if it needs adjusting:

Attitude Determines My Day

I woke up early today, excited over all I get to do before the clock strikes midnight; I have responsibilities to fulfill today. I am important. What today will be like is up to me. I get to choose what kind of day I will have!

Today I can complain because the weather is rainy, or I can be thankful that the grass is getting watered for free.

Today I can feel sad that I don't have more money, or I can be glad that my finances encourage me to plan my purchases wisely and guide me away from waste.

Today I can grumble about my health, or I can rejoice that I am alive.

Today I can lament over all that my parents didn't give me when I was growing up, or I can feel grateful that they allowed me to be born.

Today I can cry because roses have thorns, or I can celebrate that thorns have roses.

Today I can mourn my lack of friends, or I can excitedly embark upon a quest to discover new relationships and rekindle old ones.

Today I can whine because I have to go to work, or I can shout for joy because I have a job to do.

Today I can complain because I have to go to school, or I can eagerly open my mind and fill it with new tidbits of knowledge.

Today I can murmur dejectedly because I have to do housework, or I can feel honored because the Lord has provided shelter for my mind, body and soul.

Today stretches ahead of me waiting to be shaped, and here I am, the sculptor who gets to do the shaping

Set Sail for Adventure!

Lighten up. Don't take life so seriously.

Pick a day to fly a kite together. The beach or a meadow is a beautiful kite-flying setting for making memories.

Spend a weekend away together – consider taking board games.

Go barefoot in the park. (Rent this movie and watch it together).

Read the book, *Dangerous Wonder* by Mike Yaconelli and learn what it means to have childlike faith.

Plan a gourmet meal. Go to the grocery together to shop for the necessary ingredients. That evening, prepare your candlelight dinner, turn down the lights, add some romantic music, honor one another with a toast – and celebrate!

Explore new ways the two of you can celebrate together.

Celebrate your life.

Celebrate your marriage.

Remember that life is a mystery to be lived – not a problem to be solved.

Finally, celebrate your safe passage through The Seven C's of Marriage! Pat one another on the back; give a big, warm hug to one another. You have been through some rough seas and you have endured. Celebrate!

Celebration
Ponder Page...

1. Do you celebrate your marriage with a balance of grace and truth?
   What are some of the ways you celebrate?

2. Do you feel free to celebrate together with child-like enthusiasm? If not, why not?

3. If you do not feel free to get in touch with your inner child, how can your spouse help?

4. Are you a safe place for one another?

5. How can you celebrate as a couple on a weekly basis? List your ideas.

The Essential C

CHRIST

He died to set you free!

He lives in you today!

When you need Him, He is always there.

You need Him every minute of every day!

Chapter Eight

Christ – The Essential C

Keeping the Faith

Peter and Ruth were in their mid-thirties when they met. "It took many years to learn God's plan for us," says Ruth. "Many years and many tears. We had both experienced the crushing pain of abusive relationships in our former marriages and gone through the guilt and humiliation of divorce. Neither of us had ever known the joy of a Christ-centered relationship until He brought us together."

While still a teenager, Ruth married her high school sweetheart. "My parents disapproved of Jim. They sensed his wild streak, but I found him exciting. I didn't think I could live without him." From the beginning, Jim's power over Ruth was complete. While Ruth dreamed only of being a wife and mother, Jim wanted her to be his smart, sexy party girl – a drinking partner on weekends and a moneymaker the rest of the time, bringing in more than her share of the finances. "Party hardy, look pretty, and work hard – that was my life, but it seemed that no matter how hard I tried to please Jim, I always fell short." It wasn't long before Jim's wild streak turned mean. "When he drank, which was often, his verbal and physical abuse was extreme."

Not wanting her parents to know what she was suffering at the hands of her husband, Ruth became distant from family and friends, isolated in a world of turmoil and pain. Often, she thought of escaping. A few times, she actually left him, but always returned. "He would tell me it was all my fault and I believed him. I always ended up apologizing to him. I kept thinking if I'd just done something different, he wouldn't have lost control and hurt me."

When Ruth got pregnant, complications forced her into bed-rest. "Jim was so angry that I couldn't do anything with him, and that I wasn't working and making money. He would leave and stay away for days." When Ruth lost the baby several months into her pregnancy, Jim did not share in her grief. In fact, he continued to ignore her needs, leaving her to deal with the loss by herself.

"That was when I finally turned to God," she recalls. "Even in the darkest times, I'd known He was there, but Jim was against going to church, so I had stopped going. After I lost the baby, I began attending church again in spite of his disapproval. I kept praying that God would intervene in our marriage and I kept trying to please Jim, but the stronger my faith became, the angrier he got."

Ruth's second pregnancy began with similar complications. Although doctors advised against it, she was determined to carry her baby full-term this time, even if it took complete bed-rest. She spent her pregnancy praying. Friends at church laid hands on her and prayed with her. Jim remained distant, concerned only with his own desires, which were not being met. When she gave birth to a healthy daughter, Ruth rejoiced, but Jim didn't seem to care about the baby. Ruth continued to do everything she could to save her marriage, but following an especially severe beating by her husband, she finally decided that divorce was her only recourse. *"I believed divorce was a sin. But my life had become a living hell. I was afraid for myself and my baby."*

Faced with the prospect of divorce, Jim tormented Ruth endlessly. He warned her that she couldn't survive without him; that no one else would ever want her; that she would be left high and dry, even though he was financially able to pay child support. For years following the divorce, Ruth and her child lived in poverty, while Jim continued to grow his business and prosper.

In spite of only paying child support when forced to do so by the court and maintaining an immoral lifestyle that included heavy drinking, Jim insisted on his parental rights and the same court backed him up, allowing him to take his daughter for visitation regularly. *"Many times, I stayed on my knees praying the whole time she was in Jim's custody. In the meantime, it was as if God was working a puzzle in my heart – gently putting back the pieces of my life that had been scattered for so long. He restored my relationship with my family. That was one piece. He restored my finances with a good job. He gave me a healthy child and creative ways to teach her, in spite of the destructive times she spent with her dad. He surrounded me with Godly friends. The missing piece was Peter."*

Peter was in his mid-twenties when he got married for all the wrong reasons. *"I didn't want to be alone. Family was important to me and when I met an older woman with two children who wanted to marry me, I was ready. I thought she needed me."* Even though he knew *about his wife's marijuana use prior to their marriage, Peter was certain he could change her. After all, he attended church regularly and his faith in God was strong. It was just a matter of time before God would heal her of her addiction. In the meantime, Peter finally had the family he craved.*

It didn't take long for him to realize that his bride was deceitful. "She lied about her age. She lied about being able to have more children – she couldn't," he says. "Within a couple of years, I discovered that in addition to the heavy marijuana use, she had long been addicted to prescription drugs."

For the next twelve years, in spite of the deceptions, Peter devoted himself to his marriage, his role as a father, his job as a journalist, and his church. "I never missed church, sang in the choir, and my oldest daughter, Cary, was the child of my heart. She loved going to church with me, and the others would go occasionally."

It was when Peter found evidence that his wife was having an affair that his world began to fall apart. "Even though she denied it, I knew, but divorce was not what I wanted. With all my heart, I wanted to save my marriage and keep my family." For the next two years, Peter sought spiritual help with a Christian healing ministry. "My counselors helped me see something in the spiritual realm that I had never seen before. On the day I discovered incontrovertible evidence of my wife's affair, as tears ran down my face, Jesus was sitting there next to me, his arms surrounding me as He cried, too. That sustained me."

It was during this troubled time in his life that Peter received an assignment to interview Evangelist Billy Graham. While waiting at an airport for the famous man of God to arrive, Peter noted that Mrs. Graham, seated in a wheelchair, was also waiting for her husband to emerge from the airplane. "When Dr. Graham saw his wife, Ruth, their eyes locked. He saw no one but her as he rushed toward her and held her face in his hands and kissed her with such gentleness and love. I thought to myself, 'That is what I want and that is what I don't have.'"

Peter filed for divorce the following month. Lonely and yearning for love, he soon found himself entangled in an intimate relationship with a woman in his church. "It was wrong," he said. "I turned to human comfort rather than the comfort of God, and it almost destroyed me." On the day his divorce became final, the woman ended their relationship.

Peter was a broken man. He could not face returning to his church. He was struggling financially as a result of the divorce. Emotionally and spiritually, he was bankrupt. Sinking into a deep, clinical depression, he began drinking, chain-smoking and skipping meals. Within months, he had lost 50 pounds. Weak and barely functioning, his world completely turned upside down, Peter was hit with still another blow when his beloved step-daughter, Cary, died. "I would pray to God each night to take my life and be angry at Him every morning when I woke up and was still here."

In the meantime, for over nine years, Ruth had focused on her child, her church and her career. During much of that time, she had spent many hours in prayer with Don and Anne. "With the help of God, and with laughter and love laced with prayer, Don and Anne brought me through many rough times. I consider them my spiritual parents, so it was natural for me to go to them for advice when finally I realized that my healing would not be complete until there was a man in my life – a very special man."

What Ruth didn't know was that her future husband was already her friend – a man at her church named Peter; a very special man who had recently gone through a painful divorce and was attending her Singles Class.

"I knew from the moment I stumbled – and I do mean stumbled - into that church and heard the beautiful praise music that I was on the path to recovery," says Peter. "I was so hungry, I joined the praise choir, the singles class, the divorce care class, and, finally, the Disciple One Class. There, we studied Old Testament prophets and learned how God talked to the people of Israel and told them He loved them and wanted to restore them to their homeland even though they had sinned grievously. My Bible has notes all over the place in Isaiah and Jeremiah, which outline true historical events but are also metaphors for people who are hurting. God does want to restore us to wholeness. He has a plan for each of us and He knows the plan. It's a beautiful plan."

Part of God's plan for Peter was that he would attend a Sunday School Class on the Song of Solomon, dealing very bluntly with the issues of sex outside of marriage, dating and all of the worldly challenges associated with it. "Most of my relationships with women had been sexual," he admits. "This class was like nothing I'd ever studied before. I determined that if I was ever to have a successful relationship, it had to be chaste until marriage." But was he destined to ever have a successful relationship? He had female friends at church, like Ruth who sang next to him in the choir, but where was his soul mate? For now, he had his friends at work and at church and he had his dog, Maxwell, who had been there through the worst of times. *"Maxwell was a mutt with an angelic smile on his face. In fact, I believe he was one of God's angels."*

When Max died of cancer, Peter missed choir for the first time. Ruth called to make sure he was alright and when he told her about Maxwell, she prayed with him on the phone and suggested they go out for coffee. *"We talked for hours – about everything."* Peter grinned. *"We haven't missed a day of talking and praying with one another since then."*

A loving relationship centered in Christ and based on prayer evolved. Never has a couple been so in love and so in sync. When Peter and Ruth began making a list of wedding guests, they prayed over each name, asking God to take away pain and intervene in their lives – just as He has done in theirs. Their wedding ceremony was a triumphant testimony to the strength and compassion that comes from putting Christ in the middle of a relationship. Before they exchanged wedding vows, Don Bloch gave his homily called Sailing the Seven C's of Marriage, the C's being Covenant, Commitment, Communication, Compassion, Conflict, Cost, and Celebration ... with Christ at the helm.

"Peter and I vowed to save sex for marriage. We were certain we would be compatible physically. We knew that we could face whatever challenges arose. We realized there would be a period of adjustment in combining two households and living together as man and wife, with a teenager to boot, but we left it in God's hands. When it is God's will, it just happens naturally. Our bond is unbreakable. Peace and joy - that's what we've found together, "says Ruth. "We know now that the first thing to do is build a relationship with God. Know that He is a God of love, compassion and mercy. He shed every tear with me and felt every pain I felt until I fully gave myself to Him and prayed for exactly what I needed through Him. He gave His word that He would restore us, and that the old would fall away, and it has. Peter and I have been given the desires of our heart. The puzzle is complete."

"God put us together – there's no question in my mind," declares Peter. *"I remember when I saw Billy and Ruth Graham look at one another. After fifty years of marriage to my Ruth, I will still look at her that way, and I know, without a shadow of a doubt, that if I'm still here in fifty years, that's how she will look at me."*

The Love Press

Abby was engaged but she had her doubts about her fiancé. He just didn't share Abby's deep faith in God. Their relationship was filled with conflict. A friend suggested that Abby counsel with Don and Anne. "You can trust them with your life," her friend told her. "They'll be honest with you and tell it like it is." At first, Abby brought her fiancé with her to see Don and Anne, but by the third session, he refused to go and Abby came to the appointment alone. That relationship was finished.

"Don and Anne redirected me," says Abby. "They helped me heal some broken pieces in my life. I'd been married four times and needed to learn who I was as a daughter of the Lord before I gave my heart to another man. They knew my heart's desire was to be married to a man who loved the Lord more than he loved me, and they began praying with me for a God-loving husband." Don had visualized a ring on Abby's hand. He told her that he was certain that God had chosen a husband for her.

One night, Abby got invited by some old friends from junior high school to a local pub where some other school friends were playing in a band. "I moved away when I was a sophomore in high school and hadn't seen some of these friends for 37 years," she recalls. One of the guys singing with the band was Jack, the older brother of Bill, a boy Abby had a crush on in junior high. On a break, Abby told Jack and his wife, Mary, about the days she used to sit on the bulkhead in Jacksonville Beach and watch Bill surf. "We were as serious as an 11 and 12 year-old can be, until Bill broke up with me for another girl," laughed Abby. Later, Mary came up to Abby and said, "Bill's here." Sure enough, he was up on stage playing a guitar.

Their eyes met in recognition and as soon as he came down from the stage, they began talking. Abby noticed that Bill was wearing a bracelet that had "Christ Follower" on it – a reference to Matthew 9:9. When she pointed it out, Bill responded, "If you only knew what God has done for me and how much I love the Lord." That statement hit Abby like a ton of bricks! Could this be the husband God had chosen for her? They danced and talked the night away.

"It was like being with my best friend," says Abby. "And there was this overwhelming feeling of the Holy Spirit surrounding us. Bill didn't call me for three days. When he called, he said, "I don't know if you feel it, but something is happening."

Bill had been praying for a Godly woman, just as Abby had been praying for a man who loved the Lord. Their first date was to church. It was during the Easter season and they decided to let the Lord lead them in their relationship. Within three months, they were engaged, but Abby wanted to be sure this time. As a 50 year old musician, Bill had developed a drinking habit, and Abby felt that Don and Anne could help him stop drinking alcohol. "It was something I needed to do and praying about it with Abby, and Don and Anne helped me get sober and stay that way," says Bill.

It was a year before Abby and Bill got married and during that year, they met regularly with Don and Anne, and Bill attended AA. As they marked their two year wedding anniversary in 2013, Bill marked his three year anniversary of sobriety. "We were two lonely people yearning for a Christian relationship. Abby was a Godsend, literally."

Today, Abby and Bill rely on keeping Christ in the center of their marriage. Every day, they do what they have named "The Love Press." "We press into the Lord and He presses into us," says Abby. "We have overwhelming love for one another through the Holy Spirit. If either of us ever feels a little distant from the other, we pray right away for The Love Press, and it just gets better and better."

II Corinthians 5:17-18: *Therefore, if anyone is in Christ, he is a new creation; the old has gone, the new has come! All this is from God, who reconciled us to Himself through Christ and gave us the ministry of reconciliation.*

It is our belief that one of God's purposes for the Cross can be summed up in this passage. It also applies to our vertical relationship with God and the horizontal relationship to and with our spouse. We have mentioned earlier that at the wedding ceremony, two shall become one; that we move from selfishness to selflessness, and we move from mine to ours. The OLD has gone! The NEW has come! Thank you, God!

What Jesus did for us on the Cross was to reconcile us back to the Father, and through Christ, we were all given the ministry of reconciliation. This includes our relationship with our spouse. We are called to be reconcilers.

As we began to ask God what to include in this final chapter, we found ourselves back in Boulder, Colorado at the home of our daughter, Anne, and her husband, Bob, celebrating life! There are now two additions to their family, daughter Grace and son Henry. We have returned to the beginning! This is where the "Seven C's of Marriage" was birthed! Christ gave the Seven C's Homily to us especially so that we could use it in officiating at their wedding. And now, to share with you:

(Don): As I sit at the dining room table viewing the beautiful flat iron mountain ridge in the distance, I also see the meadow in the back yard and the patio where their wedding took place that warm August afternoon. It is amazing to us how we have come full circle. And how this complete circle is one of the symbols of the wedding ring. It is God's plan. There is no beginning and no end to the complete circle, just as there is no beginning and no end to the love God gives us for one another – especially in marriage.

There are many scriptures to confirm God's desires and the blessings He bestows upon husbands and wives. I believe His entire book is about the coming marriage and celebration of the bride, the church, and the groom, Jesus Christ. Many of the stories Jesus told relate to the Biblical customs of marriages. If you seek you will find other Biblical references that can apply to God's plan for marriage.

146

(Anne): I am sitting here reminiscing on the very patio, in the very month Don and I had the honor of marrying our beloved Anne and Bob. As the Colorado sun warms my face, the memories of that day warm my heart. I had promised Anne for several months prior to the wedding that I would not cry. However, the very moment she appeared, the tears began to flow and continued throughout the ceremony. One of the guests who did not know I was the Mother of the Bride said, "Where in the world did they find that emotional woman?" When I pronounced them husband and wife, my words were, "With all my love, and with great honor, I proudly present to you Mr. and Mrs. Robert Redford." It may help here to explain that Bob greatly resembles the actor Robert Redford, sounds just like him and is blessed with his same calm demeanor.

When we arrived at the Boulderado Hotel, Bob and Anne's friends had changed the Marquee from Hedlund (their actual last name) to "Redford Wedding Reception." They turned my faux pas into fun! Their friends have nicknamed Anne and Bob's home "Sundance" ... more fun.

On a more serious note, it was at their wedding reception that I experienced the blessing of closure with my first husband, Anne's father, when I asked him to forgive me for any hurts I had caused him. He has never asked me to forgive him ... that's between him and God.

Another heart-warming memory of that day is the image of my precious daughter, Bunni, simply beautiful as Matron-of-honor. Her three daughters, Lindsey, Maddie and Megan were delightful as flower girls. The four of them are a treasured part of our wedding memories.

When Don and I were married, our Lord inspired me to write a wedding song. I sang it to Don during our wedding ceremony and, with slight revision, recited it to Anne and Bob on their wedding day. In 2013, I also had the pleasure of reciting it when we married our daughter Bunni to John Moore. I share it here, with you, in prayer that your journey on the Seven C's will be blessed with the joy that we have experienced:

Our Wedding Song

My beloved Don, on this our wedding day
we are one forever more to stay.
We know God intended it this way
and our lives are one in Him, to stay
on this our wedding day.

I do pledge my love to you this day
my dreams to you this day
my trust in you this day,
my faith in you this day
and I pledge my life to you
on this our wedding day.

I will love you more than yesterday
and less than tomorrow,
every day in every way.
on this our wedding day,
on this our wedding day.

Epilogue

By Anne Bloch

As two people who have been to the valley and the mountaintop, we have been groomed by God to minister to couples at every conceivable level of a relationship – and we do mean EVERY. Since Don and I are both parents of children of divorce, we know the terrible hurt and rejection felt from both sides. This helps us help others with a deeper understanding.

Together, we decided to go back to college to earn our doctorates in Pastoral Ministry. Today, people have fun calling us "the marriage doctors." It is ONLY through the unconditional love of GOD, the healing love of JESUS and the guidance of the HOLY SPIRIT that our ministry has helped marriages as well as those contemplating marriage. What a blessing it is for us to have the privilege of doing pre-marital counseling with couples. It gives us the opportunity to bond with them. Many life-long friendships have been birthed. Some even ask us to marry them. What an honor!

One of the many blessings for us in being in this ministry is the awesome privilege of seeing God work in the lives of His beloved children.

Remember, putting Christ in the center of your marriage and your life is our goal and His. When Satan knocks at the door, simply say, "Jesus, will you please get that for me?" He will, gladly. He was hoping you would ask.

Jesus gave me a wonderful discovery. Since our thought-life is Satan's battleground, a good trick to play on him when he decides to bring up our past, is to say, "Thank you, Satan, for reminding me of that. It reminds me to thank Jesus once again for His healing grace in that area of my life!" You will find that Satan's evil bombardments will be fewer each time you go to Jesus with thanksgiving.

Jesus is waiting to be invited into your marriage. It is time to give up control of the helm to your Lord. Together, drop to your knees, confess your shortcomings, let Jesus know how much you need Him now and always, in all ways.

One on a Seesaw

Several years ago, we facilitated a church group made up of men and (mostly) women who had a spouse sitting at home who was not interested in making the marriage work. However, they did not want to head for the divorce courts either. It was the age-old, worn out myth that "I still love you, I'm just not in love anymore." Anne came up with a terrific title of our newly formed group and called it "One on a Seesaw." I remember it as a "Teeter-Totter" says Anne with a sigh. "Sure makes me feel old." If you have ever attempted being on a seesaw by yourself, you get the image.

With permission from Alcoholics Anonymous we compiled a Twelve Step Program for our group. This accomplished a new insight and led the participants to stop trying to change their spouse. Instead, they learned to focus on themselves. We mentioned this program on the Smartmarriages.com Website and received requests for Twelve Step copics World-Wide. E-mail was received from Singapore, South Africa, and throughout Europe, South America and the United States. The following is the Twelve Step Program compiled for those who are currently sailing solo. If this applies to you, we pray it guides you into God's safe harbor. Bon voyage!

TWELVE STEPS for ONE ON A SEESAW

STEP ONE
We admitted we were powerless over a lot of what happens in our marital relationships, and that our lives could become unmanageable.

STEP TWO
Came to believe that God can change us and restore us to wholeness.

STEP THREE
Made a decision to turn our will and our lives over to the care of God and to confess that it is NOT our responsibility to change our spouse — nor do we have that right or power.

STEP FOUR
Made a searching and fearless moral inventory of ourselves asking the Holy Spirit to convict us of our shortcomings.

STEP FIVE
Admitted to God to ourselves, and one other person the exact nature of our wrongs.

STEP SIX
Were entirely ready to have God, through His grace and mercy, remove all these defects of character.

STEP SEVEN
Humbly asked Jesus Christ through His unconditional love and forgiveness to help us remove our shortcomings.

STEP EIGHT
Made a list of all the ways we may have harmed our spouse and became willing to make amends to them through asking for forgiveness and repenting.

STEP NINE
Made direct amends to our spouse whenever possible, except where to do so would cause them harm.

STEP TEN
Continued to take personal inventory and when we were wrong, promptly admitted it.

STEP ELEVEN
Sought through prayer and meditation to improve our conscious contact with God, praying for knowledge of God's will for us and to receive the power of The Holy Spirit to carry this out.

STEP TWELVE
Having had a spiritual awakening as a result of these steps, we agreed to carry this message to other hurting marital relationships and to practice these principals in all our endeavors.

(Adapted From The Twelve Steps of A.A.) Disclaimer: The Twelve steps of Alcoholics Anonymous have been reprinted and adapted with the permission of Alcoholics Anonymous World Services, Inc. ("A.A.W.S). Permission to reprint and adopt the Twelve Steps does not mean that Alcoholics Anonymous is affiliated with this program. A.A. is a program of recovery from alcoholism only — use of A.A.'s steps or an adapted version of its Steps in connection with programs and activities which are patterned after A.A., but which addresses other problems, or use in any other non-A.A. context, does not imply otherwise. Additionally, while A.A. is a spiritual program, A.A. is not a religious program. Thus, A.A. is not affiliated or allied with any sect, denomination, or specific religious belief.

Life Preservers:

No digging up the past.

No blaming your spouse.

Eliminate expectations of your spouse. Look inward. *What can I change about myself?*

Eliminate the word "but" in communicating and replace it with "and."

Communicate using "I" statements rather than "you" statements.

Give up control. Take a risk ... be vulnerable.

Discover one another's love language.

Share your needs – honor your partner's needs.

Love unconditionally. "Love one another as I have loved you." (John 13:34)

Forgive as God forgives you.

Pray together every day.

Pronounce a daily blessing upon your spouse (and your children, if you have them).

Always have Jesus Christ at the center of your relationship.

We fervently pray for God's Blessings upon your current marriage or your upcoming wedding. Remember, the wedding is merely an event on one particular day. The marriage will take place the rest of your lives with Father, Son and Holy Spirit. God bless you now and always as you embark on your journey together with Jesus Christ as your compass.

Celebrate!

Susan D. Brandenburg
Co-Author

Award-winning biographer Susan D. Brandenburg was honored to co-author this important book with her blessed brother and sister in Christ, Don and Anne Bloch. Susan's words are a gift from God. She thanks Him daily for allowing her to help preserve the legacies of His children. It is Susan's prayer that this book will be a best-seller that takes the nation and globe by storm and heals the marriages of millions of couples by helping them put Jesus Christ at the helm as they Sail the Seven C's!

Andie Jackson
Graphic Designer

*P*roud to have been included in the creation of this excellent book, Andrea "Andie" Jackson has been continually employed in the field of printing since 1984, and as a graphic designer since the early nineties. For the last six years, for as many projects, she has been blessed to work with her beautiful, talented, dear friend and honorary sister, Susan D. Brandenburg. Through Susan, Andie came to know Don and Anne Bloch, and during the progress of this book *Sail the Seven Seas of Matrimony,* has come to love and admire them. Their dedication to the Godly vocation of marriage counseling and to the Christian values they exhibit in daily life is an inspiration.

Some Suggested Resources:

WEBSITES

www.smalley.gospel.net (Smalley Ministries)
www.smartmarriages.com (Diane Sollee)
www.family.org/married (Focus on the Family)
www.marriagesavers.com (Marriage Savers)
www.utahmarriage.org (Marriage topics archives)
www.encounter.org (Marriage Encounter)
www.bettermarriages.org (Marriage Enrichment)
www.reconcilinggodsway.com (Marriages in trouble)
www.retrouvaille.org (Marriages in trouble)
www.ocmarriage.org (Marriage topics archives)
www.famtoday.com (Jimmy Evans Ministry: Marriage on the Rock.)
www.greatcommandment.net (Intimate Life Ministries/Intimate Encounters)
www.pairs.com (Practical Application of Intimate Relationship Skills)

PREMARITAL/MARITAL EVALUATIONS

FOCCUS, INC.
Nazarus Hall, 3300 North 60th Street
Omaha, NE. 68104-3495

PREPARE/ENRICH
P.O. Box 190
Minneapolis, MN. 55440-0190

Selected Bibliography:

Anderson, Neil T. & Charles Mylander. *The Christ Centered Marriage*. Regal Books. 1996.

Chapman, Gary. *Toward a Growing Marriage*. Chicago, IL. Moody Press. 1998.

Clinton, Dr. Tim. *Before a Bad Goodbye: How to Turn Your Marriage Around*. Word Publishing. 1999.

Cloud, Dr. Henry & Dr. John Townsend. *Boundaries in Marriage*. Zondervan Publishing House. 1999.

Covey, Stephen R. *The Seven Habits of Highly Effective Families*. Golden Books. 1997.

Davis, Michele Weiner. *The Divorce Remedy*. Simon & Schuster. 2001.

Davis, Will, Jr. *Pray Big For Your Marriage*. Grand Rapids, MI. Revell. 2008.

Evans, Jimmy. *Our Secret Paradise*. Ventura, CA. Regal Books. 2006.

Ferguson, Dr. David & Dr. Don McMinn. *Top 10 Intimacy Needs*. Intimacy Press. 1994.

Gordon, Lori H. *Passage to Intimacy*. Simon & Schuster. 1993.

Guernsey, Dennis B. *The Family Covenant: Love and Forgiveness*. David Cook Publishing. 1984.

Hill, Craig S. *Marriage: Covenant or Contract*. Northglenn, CO. Harvest Books and Publishing. 1992.

Intimate Life Ministries. *Experiencing God in Marriage, Family, and The Church*. Intimacy Press. 1995.

Logan, James. *Reclaiming Surrendered Ground*. Chicago, IL. Moody Press. 1995.

MacDonald, James. *Seven Words to Change Your Family...While There's Still Time.* Moody Press. 2002.

Markman, J. *Fighting For Your Marriage.* 2001.
     Marriage Savers. MI. Zondervan Publishing House. 1993.

McCain, Savanna & Milt Bryan. *A Lasting Promise; A Christian Guide to Fighting For Your Marriage.* Jossey-Bass Publishers. 1998.

McManus, Michael & Harriet McManus. *Living Together, Myths, Risks & Answers.* New York. Howard Books. 2008.

Notarius, Clifford, Ph.D. & Howard Markman, Ph.D. *We Can Work it Out.* Penguin Putnam, Inc. 1993.

Olson, David & Amy K. Olson. *Empowering Couples.* Life Innovations, Inc. 2000.

Parsons, Rob. *The Sixty Minute Marriage Builder.* TN. Broadman & Holman Publishers. 1998.

Parrott, Drs. Les & Leslie. *When Bad Things Happen to Good Marriages.* Grand Rapids, MI. Zondervan Publishing House. 2001.

Parrott, Drs. Les & Leslie. *Saving Your Marriage Before it Starts.* MI. Zondervan Publishing House. 1995.

Rainey, Dennis, David Boehi, Brent Nelson, Jeff Schulte & Lloyd Shadrach. *Preparing For Marriage.* Ventura, CA. Gospel Light. 1997.

Rosen, Margery D. *Seven Secrets of a Happy Marriage.* Workman Publishing Co. 2002.

Smalley, Gary. *For Better or For Best.* MI. Zondervan Publishing House. 1982.
     If Only He Knew. MI. Zondervan Publishing House. 1979.
     Making Love Last Forever. Word Publishing. 1996.

www.ingramcontent.com/pod-product-compliance
Lightning Source LLC
Chambersburg PA
CBHW081511040426
42447CB00013B/3188